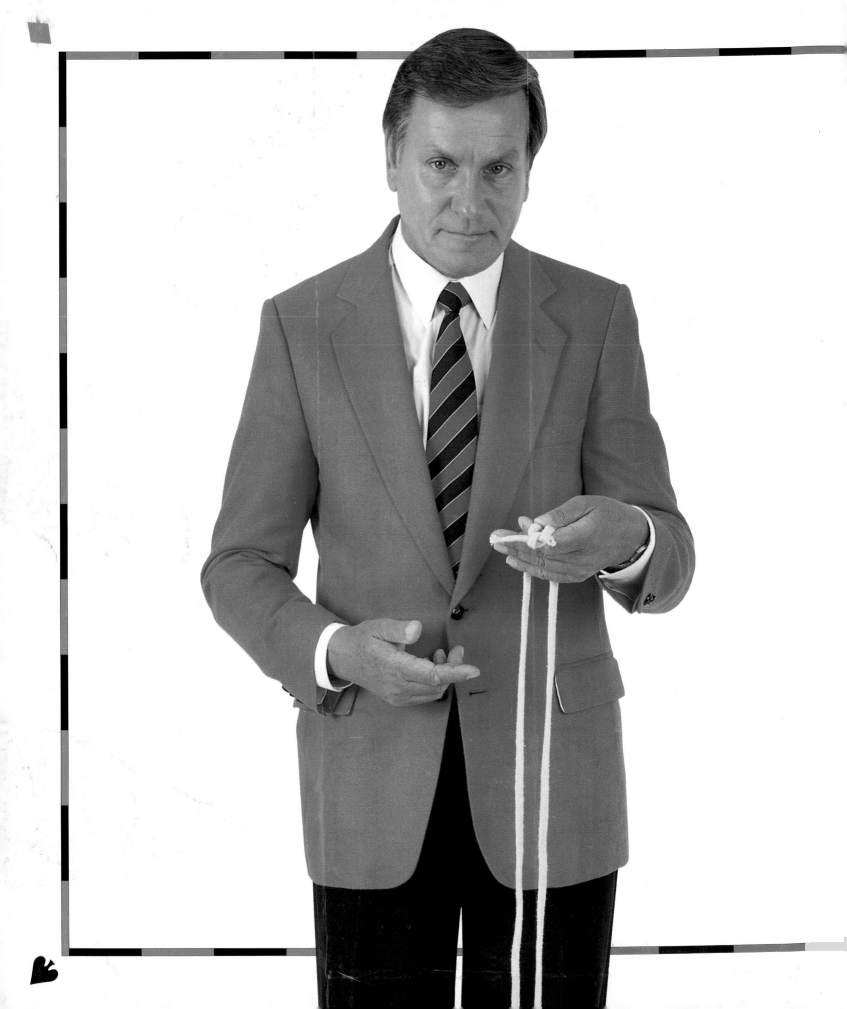

THE AMAZING BOOK OF

MAGIC

A STEP-BY-STEP ILLUSTRATED GUIDE
TO A HOST OF SIMPLE YET SPECTACULAR TRICKS

JON TREMAINE

Bramley
Books

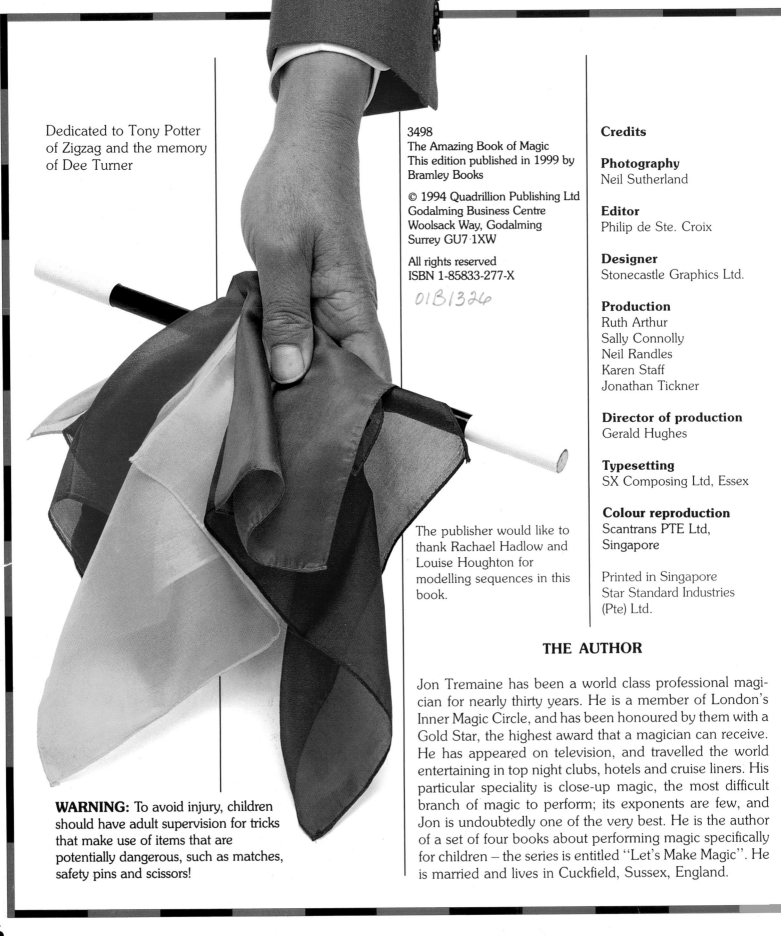

Dedicated to Tony Potter
of Zigzag and the memory
of Dee Turner

3498
The Amazing Book of Magic
This edition published in 1999 by
Bramley Books

© 1994 Quadrillion Publishing Ltd
Godalming Business Centre
Woolsack Way, Godalming
Surrey GU7·1XW

01B1326

The publisher would like to
thank Rachael Hadlow and
Louise Houghton for
modelling sequences in this
book.

Credits

Photography
Neil Sutherland

Editor
Philip de Ste. Croix

Designer
Stonecastle Graphics Ltd.

Production
Ruth Arthur
Sally Connolly
Neil Randles
Karen Staff
Jonathan Tickner

Director of production
Gerald Hughes

Typesetting
SX Composing Ltd, Essex

Colour reproduction
Scantrans PTE Ltd,
Singapore

Printed in Singapore
Star Standard Industries
(Pte) Ltd.

THE AUTHOR

Jon Tremaine has been a world class professional magician for nearly thirty years. He is a member of London's Inner Magic Circle, and has been honoured by them with a Gold Star, the highest award that a magician can receive. He has appeared on television, and travelled the world entertaining in top night clubs, hotels and cruise liners. His particular speciality is close-up magic, the most difficult branch of magic to perform; its exponents are few, and Jon is undoubtedly one of the very best. He is the author of a set of four books about performing magic specifically for children – the series is entitled "Let's Make Magic". He is married and lives in Cuckfield, Sussex, England.

WARNING: To avoid injury, children should have adult supervision for tricks that make use of items that are potentially dangerous, such as matches, safety pins and scissors!

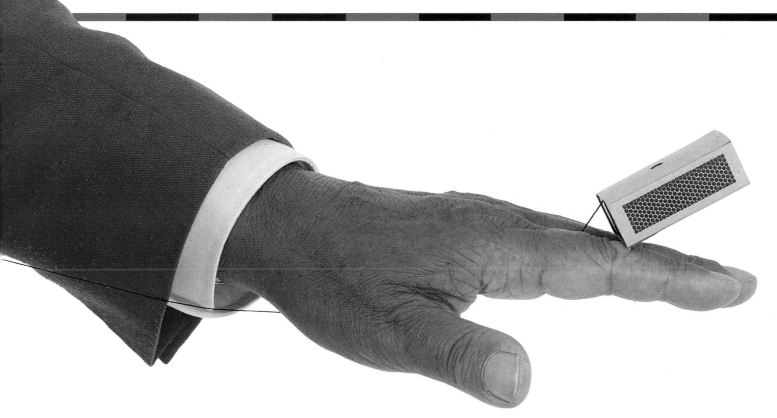

INTRODUCTION

This book, and its companion *The Amazing Book of Card Tricks*, is designed to introduce you to the fabulous world of magic. You will find that all the tricks in the following pages are easy to perform and yet will have an extraordinary effect upon your audience. Coins, paper money, safety pins, matches, rope, pens, mints, sugar cubes, newspapers, books, ash, keys and many more household items are utilized in a vast array of spectacular tricks that you will soon master.

You will be introduced to some simple elements of "sleight of hand" and will be amazed at how simple the "technical" side of the conjurer's art really is. The true art of magic lies in the *presentation*. Ninety per cent of your efforts will be taken up with acting the part of a magician. The very best magicians are almost invariably trained actors who have undergone drama tuition. I am not suggesting that you do the same – merely that you fully understand that whereas the principles are comparatively simple, the presentation of good magic is much more difficult. You will need to practise. When you have finished practising – practise again! And again!

Work on your patter (the words that you use to describe to the spectators what it is you are doing). I give suggested patter with each of the tricks. However, try to use your own words whenever possible, so that your own personality shines through and you sound more natural.

I have written this book in the sincere hope that it will encourage you to take up the noble art of magic as a hobby. It is a very nice feeling to be known as the life and soul of the party! It is a great confidence booster. When I picked my first magic book off the shelves of my local library nearly 40 years ago, I was a shy 18-year-old with an incredibly bad stammer. The stammer was so acute that acquaintances of mine who saw me coming would cross to the other side of the road in order to avoid having a conversation with me. It was that bad!

Once I started to do conjuring tricks, those same people were only too pleased to stop me in order to find out what my latest "miracle" was. They became interested in what I was doing, and consequently interested in me too. I became a professional entertainer only four years later and my stammer became a thing of the past. I can honestly say that magic changed my life. Maybe it will do the same for you. Who knows? At the very least, it will provide you with a most enjoyable and inexpensive hobby and give your friends and associates a great deal of pleasure.

PART ONE

MONEY MAGIC

COIN MAGIC

Tricks with coins are great fun to do and, as most people carry loose change around with them in their pockets and purses, most of the time you will find that you will be able to borrow the coins that you need for your tricks. The ability to palm, vanish and switch coins is a skill well worth acquiring and we are going to apply ourselves to learning these techniques now, before proceeding to the actual tricks.

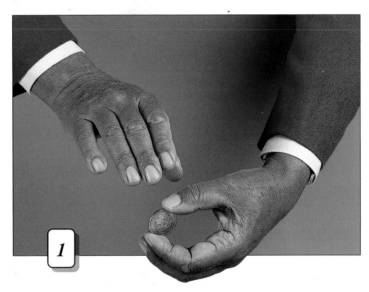

♣ VOODOO COIN VANISH ♣

It is not necessary to be a great "sleight-of-hand" expert to perform interesting and mystifying tricks. However, if you take the trouble to master this simple coin vanish, it will mean that you will be able to add a special "sparkle" to many of your coin tricks. Hold the coin in your left hand as illustrated (**1**). Your other hand travels forward to meet it, the right thumb going *under* and the right fingers going *over* the coin (**2**). Make as if to grab the coin but as soon as it is hidden from the view of the spectator by your right fingers, let the coin drop secretly into your left palm (**3**). Complete the grabbing motion with your right hand, closing it into a fist (**4**) and move the hand away (**5**). *Do not move the left hand* – merely grip the hidden coin with the second and third fingers. The right hand is now slowly opened – the coin has vanished (**6**)!

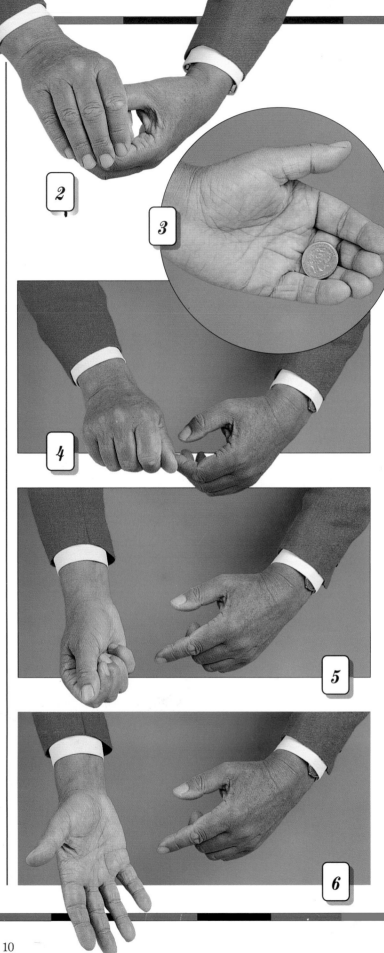

Well, that's it. Simplicity itself — but, I beg you please, please, practise this simple combination of moves until they become second nature to you. Try it in front of a mirror so that you can see how it looks from your spectators' viewpoint. You must *act* too, because if *you* do not appear to believe that the coin is in your right hand, you cannot very well expect your audience to believe it, can you?

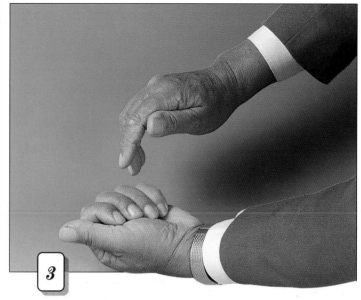

◆ PALMING A COIN ◆

Concealing objects in your hand is called "*palming*". Two simple coin palms – the finger palm and the thumb palm – will suffice for your requirements at this stage. The Voodoo Coin Vanish (above) requires you to finger palm a coin. The coin is just lightly gripped by the bent second and third fingers. The first and fourth fingers are slightly extended in a natural manner and do not actually hold the coin. Look again at picture (**3**) to understand this.

The thumb palm calls for a different type of manipulation. A coin is shown on your right palm in the position shown (**1**). You now, apparently, tip the coin into your left hand (**2**) which closes over it (**3**). On opening your left fingers, the coin is seen to have vanished (**4**). To achieve this vanish, you merely have to grip the coin in the skin fold at the base of your thumb as you turn your right hand over, as the reveal shot (**5**) shows.

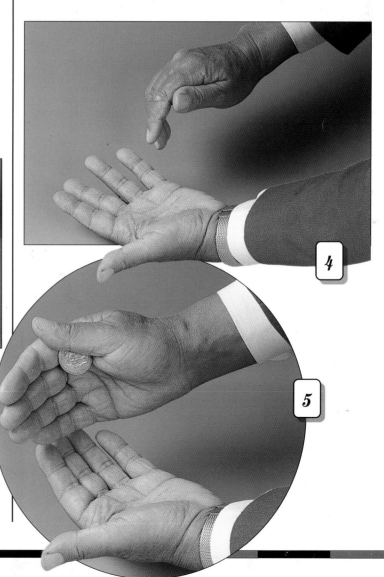

➤ THE COIN FOLD ◀

Place a coin on a square of paper as shown in picture (**1**). Now follow the sequence of actions illustrated until you have folded a packet to resemble picture (**7**). You firstly fold the paper upwards crosswise from bottom to top (**2**), then fold the left and right edges behind the coin (**3, 4, 5, 6**). Finally you fold the top flap down behind (**7**). The coin now rests in the little packet which, unknown to the spectator, is open at the top.

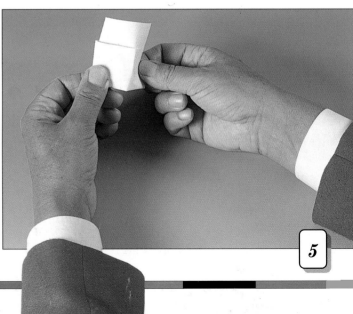

3

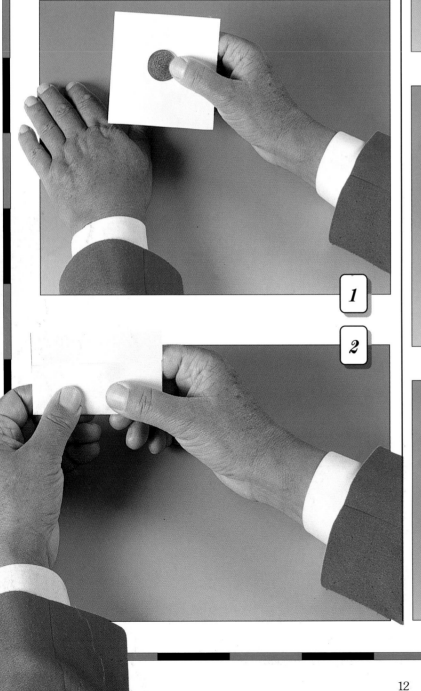

1

2

4

5

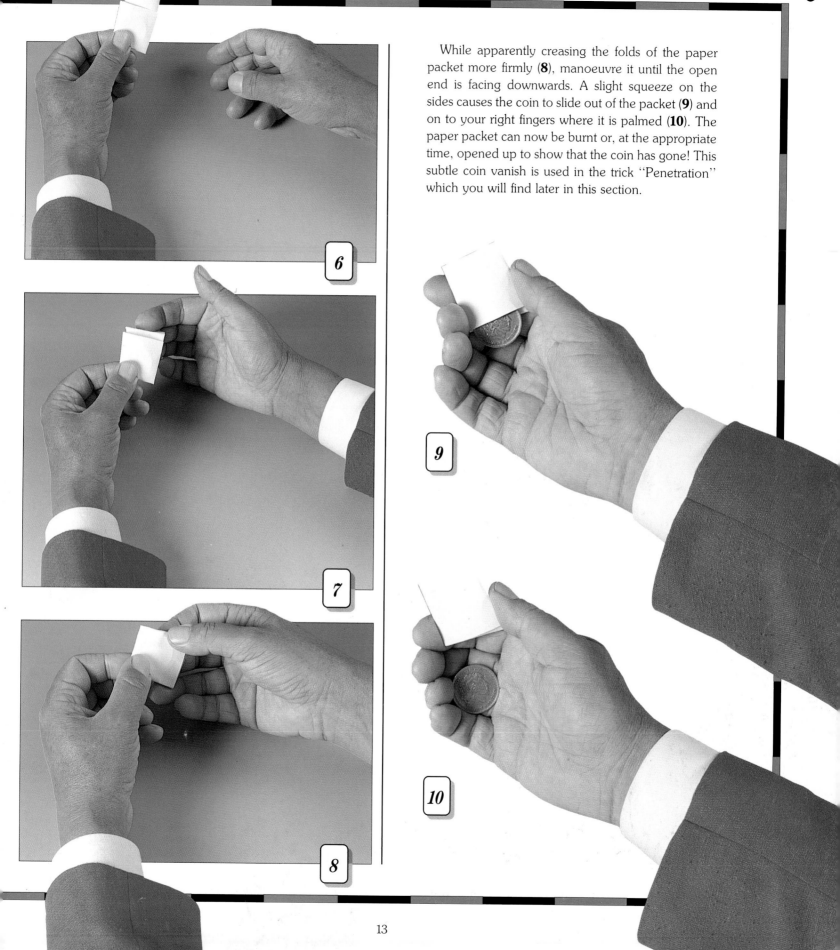

While apparently creasing the folds of the paper packet more firmly (**8**), manoeuvre it until the open end is facing downwards. A slight squeeze on the sides causes the coin to slide out of the packet (**9**) and on to your right fingers where it is palmed (**10**). The paper packet can now be burnt or, at the appropriate time, opened up to show that the coin has gone! This subtle coin vanish is used in the trick "Penetration" which you will find later in this section.

← THE SITTING-DOWN COIN VANISH →

This subtle principle can be used to vanish any small object. It is particularly suitable for coins. All sleight-of-hand actions should exactly mimic *real* actions. The closer the imitation – the greater the deception. With this thought in mind we will learn the *real* action first – the action of picking up a coin from the table!

Sit yourself with your legs tucked well under the table and your thighs pressed together. Place the coin in front of you and about 10cm from the edge of the table (**1**). Cover the coin with your right fingers and draw it towards you. As the coin reaches the edge of the table bring your thumb up so that you grasp the coin between your thumb and fingers (**2**). Close your hand into a fist and move it towards the centre of the table (**3**). Open your hand and reveal the coin (**4**).

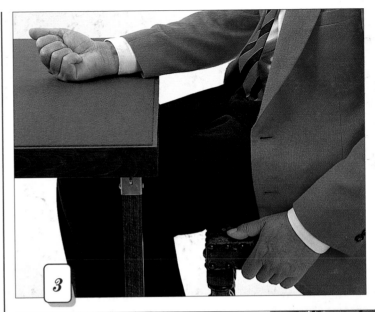

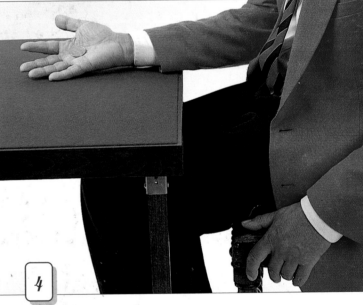

That is what you are supposed to do. Now let us look at what you actually do! When you make the coin vanish, your actions must look identical to those just described (**5**). The only difference is that as soon as the coin reaches the edge of the table (**6**), you just sweep it off and allow it to drop on to your lap (**7**). Your hand closes into a fist, as before, as if it really contained the coin and then moves forward to rest on the table (**8**). At the appropriate moment you open your hand to show that the coin has disappeared (**9**). This principle will be used with devastating effect later in a trick called "Gone".

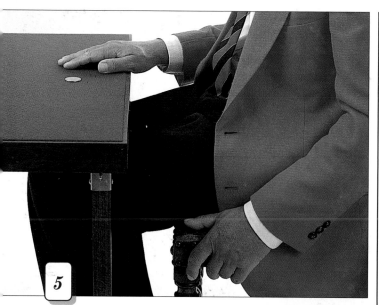

5

8

6

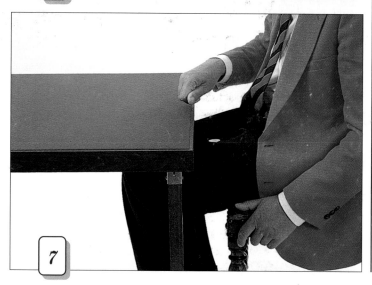

7

9

15

BRASS NECK AND ELBOW

This cheeky coin trick is as bold as brass and involves you in a routine that uses your neck and elbow – hence its unusual name.

♣ EFFECT ♣

A borrowed coin is rubbed on your left elbow and then completely vanishes! Both hands are shown empty. The right elbow is now rubbed and the coin reappears! The "Voodoo Coin Vanish" plus a wonderful subtlety (about to be explained) enable you to show both your hands empty.

REQUIREMENTS
A single coin – the bigger the better

◆ WHAT YOU DO ◆

Borrow a coin and then seat yourself at a table (**1**). Hold the coin in your left hand in the position for the "the Voodoo Vanish" but when your right hand travels forward in the action of grabbing the coin, *you actually do take it in your right hand*. Rest your head on your left hand and rub the coin on your left elbow (**2**). After a couple of seconds let the coin drop onto the table with a clatter (**3**).

Pick up the coin with your *left* hand and now repeat the above actions, only this time actually *execute* "the Voodoo Coin Vanish" taking the coin away secretly in your left hand in a finger palm position. Rest your head on your left hand again (**4**) and get rid of the coin by tucking it down the back of your collar (**5**) while your right hand is apparently rubbing it into your left elbow! Then show both hands empty. The coin has vanished (**6**)!

To make it return you have to reverse the action. Rest your head on your left hand and start rubbing your left elbow with your right fingers, as before (**7**).

6

7

8

9

10

While all the attention is drawn to your left elbow, your left fingers secretly retrieve the coin from your collar and finger palm it again.

After rubbing your elbow for a while without success you give up (**8**) and change sides – this time resting your head on your right hand and rubbing the right elbow with your left fingers (**9**). After a few rubs, let the coin drop on to the table with a clatter (**10**)! Very bewildering!

HOW COULD YOU STOOP SO LOW?

Methods in magic are unimportant! How you achieve your "miracle" is really irrelevant. The only thing that matters is the ultimate effect on the spectator. Always remember this. The method used to bring about this wonderful trick is so blatant and cheeky that you may be frightened to perform it at first. Trust me! Try it out. You will even amaze yourself!

➤ EFFECT ◄

A coin, apparently dropped accidentally, vanishes!

REQUIREMENTS
A borrowed coin

♣ WHAT YOU DO ♣

Borrow a coin and state that you will make it vanish (**1**). You make a "magic pass" over the coin and then "accidentally" (on purpose) let it drop on the floor at your feet (**2, 3**). While everyone is laughing at your clumsiness, you stoop down to retrieve the coin (**4**) but instead of picking it up, you flick it with your finger tips so that it shoots beneath your shoe (**5**)! Stand upright again with your right hand closed into a fist (**6**), as if the coin was really there. Make a "magic pass" (**7**), open your hand, the coin has vanished (**8**)! Now who's laughing?!

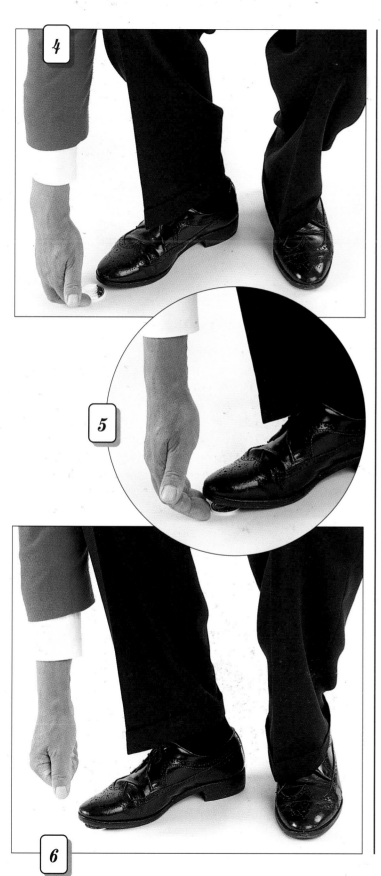

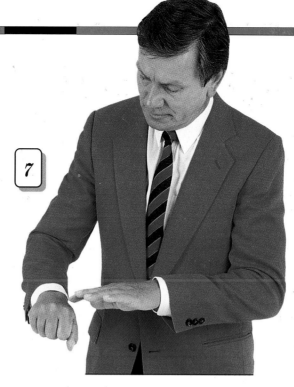

◆ AFTERTHOUGHTS ◆

If your trouser bottoms have a cuff or turn-up, you could actually pick up the coin from the floor and secretly drop it into your turn-up as you straighten up. This little refinement means you can walk off after the trick and no-one will know where the coin has gone.

THE CHEEKY COIN VANISH

This trick is so simple that a child of three could perform it (with twenty years' practice)! Seriously though, it is very cheeky indeed. Practice will make the actions smooth and the effect extremely deceptive.

◀ EFFECT ▶

A coin, apparently chosen from a handful of change, vanishes!

REQUIREMENTS
Just a handful of coins of various denominations

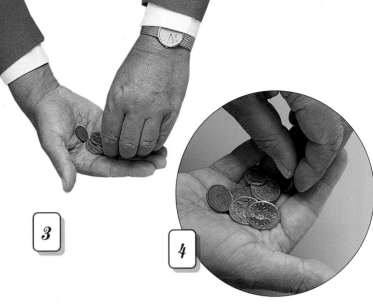

♣ WHAT YOU DO ♣

In order to perform this trick properly it is vital that the simple sequence of moves that are required of you exactly duplicate natural actions. So, first I will take you through the natural sequence.

Take all the coins out of your right pocket and display them on your right palm. Reach across with your left hand (with its back towards the spectator) and pick out one of the coins. Hold the coin between the fingers and thumb of your left hand and *at the same time* put all the other coins back in your pocket. Place the coin into your right hand, and close it into a fist. Open your hand and show the coin. This sequence of moves must be practised until it becomes smooth – second nature to you. The success of our trick depends entirely on your ability to be natural!

To make a coin vanish, you must perform all these actions, only this time, when it comes to picking up the coin – *you don't*! Yes, it is as simple as that! Remove the coins as before and display them on your palm (**1**). Reach over to take the coin with your left hand (**2**) and, as soon as the back of your hand obscures the coins from sight (**3**), *pretend* to lift out a coin, but let it slip out of your fingers again (**4**). Close your fingers over the imaginary coin and at the same time put *all* the coins back in your pocket again (**5**)! Now *pretend* to pass the coin into your right hand (**6, 7**), and make a fist (**8**). Now, at your leisure, make the imaginary coin vanish (**9**)! Both your hands are empty (**10**)! If you cannot do that, you had better give up magic and take up knitting!

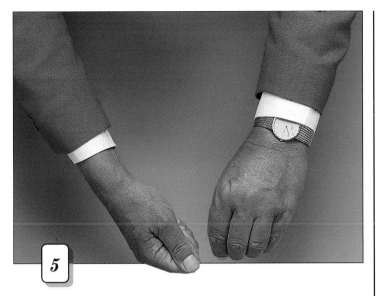

5

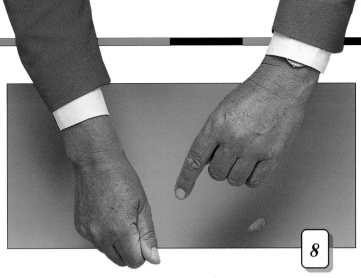

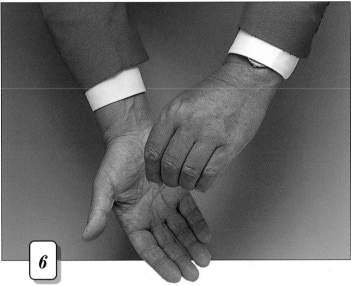

6

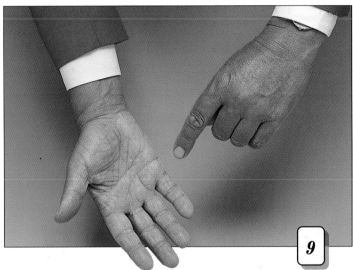

8

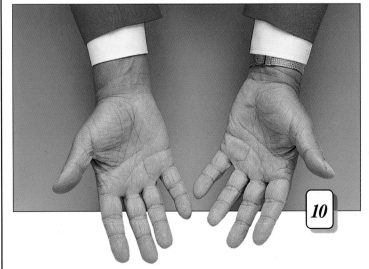

9

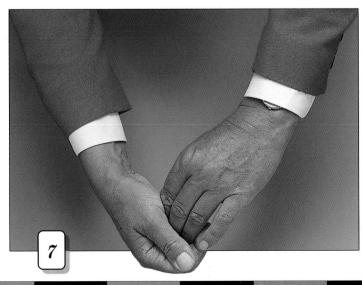

7

10

▶ AFTERTHOUGHTS ◀

Practise the sequence of moves in front of a mirror and you will see how deceptive they look. "Believe" the coin is there yourself and your audience will too!

PENETRATION

All the items required for this spectacular trick may be borrowed. No preparation is required, so it can be performed completely *impromptu*. You would be hard pressed to find a better bar or pub trick.

➤ EFFECT ◀

A borrowed, marked coin is made to pass magically into a sealed glass tumbler, in full view.

REQUIREMENTS
A glass tumbler
A drink coaster or beer mat
A coin (the larger the better)
A small piece of paper about 10cm
square – or even a banknote!
A pen

The pen will be used by the lender of the coin so that he can mark it for future identification. Coins, however, do not retain ink marks very well. Ink tends to smudge and rub off. For this reason I usually carry a strip of small, round adhesive labels in my wallet so that the spectator can stick one onto the coin and then write his initials easily upon it. Alternatively, the coin can be scratched with a knife, nail file, or similar sharp object to identify it.

◀ WHAT YOU DO ➤

Ask the spectator to loan you a coin for the trick. Try to get the largest one he has. Have him mark the coin for future identification, using whichever method best suits your situation.

"Let's wrap it up for safety"

You are now going to do the *coin fold*, as described earlier. After the folding, the packet is given a little squeeze and the coin drops on to your right fingers, which palm it (**1**). Take the packet away with your left hand and place it on the bar in full view. At the same time, with the coin still secretly concealed in your hand, pick up the coaster with your right thumb and index finger (**2**).

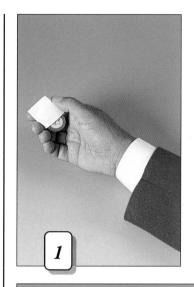

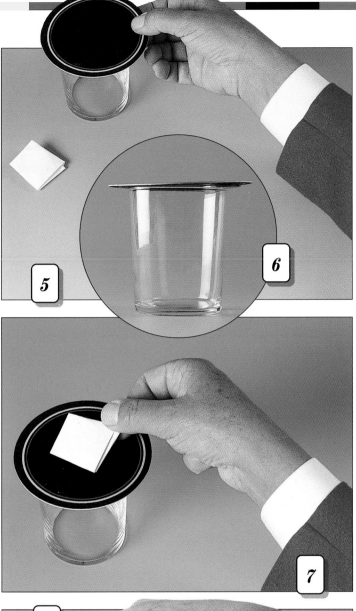

5

6

7

8

"Where's the coaster? Oh! There it is."

Turn your hand over and the coaster will automatically slide over to cover the palmed coin (**3**). Place the coaster over the mouth of the glass (**4**). In so doing, it is an easy matter to trap the coin between it and the lip of the glass (**5**)! Let go. The coin will stay in position, hidden from view (**6**), leaving your hands empty. Pick up the paper packet and place it on top of the coaster (**7**).

"Now watch closely everyone. I will show you some really penetrating magic!"

Show that your hands are empty and then give the packet a sharp tap with your finger (**8**). This will dislodge the trapped coin. It will drop visibly into the glass with a very satisfying clatter (**9**). It looks for all the world as if it has penetrated right through the paper packet and the coaster! *Don't touch anything!* Let the spectator remove the coaster and his coin from the glass. He checks his identification marks. There is no doubt about it. It is the same coin! If there is any justice in life, he will now buy you a drink!

9

♣ AFTERTHOUGHTS ♣

If you cannot find a beer mat or coaster, a pack of cards or a small book will do just as well as the "cover" for the glass.

23

HEADS YOU LOSE!

The simplest tricks are always the best – and this one is simplicity personified! Please, please *practise* until you can do the trick smoothly. If you do, you will have an absolute stunner that you will be able to perform anywhere and at any time. Get the timing right and you will be able to fool even quite knowledgeable magicians with it!

◆ EFFECT ◆

You put a coin in a spectator's hand and it completely vanishes! Then it falls out of the sky and appears in her hand again.

➤ WHAT YOU DO ◀

Stand facing the spectator with the coin in your right hand. Ask her to hold her hand out, palm upwards (**1**). Tell her that you are going to count "One" – "Two" – "Three" and on the count of "Three" she must grab the coin. If she manages to get it, she can keep it! But she must wait until you say "Three".

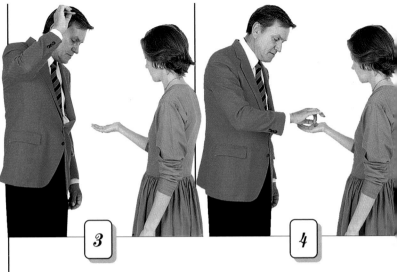

Raise your hand above your head and then bring it down again, pressing the coin on to her palm (**2**), as you count "One". Again raise your hand above your head (**3**) and bring it down, pressing the coin on to her palm (**4**), as you count "Two". Once again raise your hand (**5**), only this time *place the coin on top of your head* (**6**) . . . before bringing your hand down again as if it still contained the coin! Press your *fingers* into her palm as you count "Three". Practise this until it looks exactly like the first two times. Get a nice flowing rhythm going and she will never notice that the coin has already gone.

As soon as she hears you say "Three", she will instantly close her fingers over your fingers as she makes a grab for the coin (**7**). She may even believe that she has got it! You extract your fingers from her grip and ask her to open her fingers (**8**).

The coin has vanished!

To make the coin come back, ask her to hold her hand out again and keep staring at her empty palm. She must say to herself, "Magic Money Come Back!" *Slowly* bow your head forward. The coin will slide off the top of your head and land with a plop on her palm (**9**)! The moment it arrives on her palm, you must suddenly look upwards towards the sky as if you think that the coin must have come from somewhere up there (**10**). Open your mouth in amazement as if you can hardly believe it yourself!

A magician is really an actor playing the part of a magician – so remember to give an Oscar-winning performance!

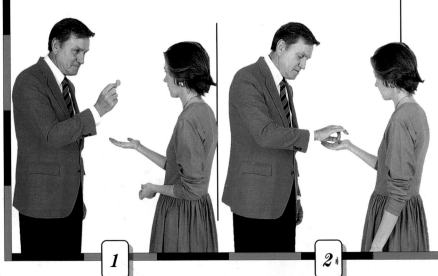

IN POCKET

You will certainly be "in pocket" if you learn to do this clever trick. It is very simple in execution but utterly bewildering to your spectators. You will need to wear a jacket or a shirt with a breast pocket to perform it, though.

◆ EFFECT ➤

An inexplicable vanish of a coin! It disappears when you cover it with a handkerchief.

<table>
<tr><td>

REQUIREMENTS
A coin (which may be borrowed)
A handkerchief or napkin

</td></tr>
</table>

✣ WHAT YOU DO ✣

Display the coin held in the fingertips of your left hand at chest level, and about 50cm in front of your body (**1**). Drape the handkerchief up and over the coin (**2, 3**). Keep pulling the handkerchief over your left hand by drawing your right hand towards your body. This hand comes to rest in line with your jacket pocket as the coin comes into view again (**4**).

Now repeat the above actions (**5**) *but* this time, as soon as your two hands come together (**6**), just grip the coin between your right finger and thumb and steal it away under cover of the handkerchief (**7**). Your right hand continues towards your top pocket as before (**8**). As soon as it reaches it, let the coin drop into your top pocket (**9**)! The handkerchief has now cleared your left hand, and the coin has vanished (**10**). Show that both hands are empty and hand the handkerchief out for examination (**11**). It's mystifying!

THE MAGIC PEN

I consider this very pretty coin trick to be worth more than the price of this book!

◆ EFFECT ◆

You hold a borrowed coin in your right fist which you tap with your "magic pen". When you open your fist, the coin has disappeared! You close your empty hand into a fist again and once more tap it with the magic pen. The coin suddenly reappears!

REQUIREMENTS
A borrowed coin
A pen with a clip top. Put the pen
into your inside jacket pocket

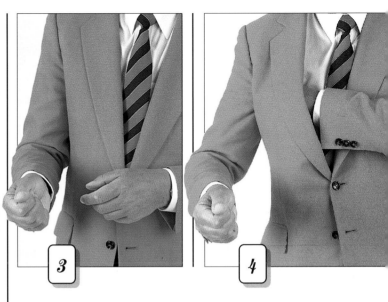

❥ WHAT YOU DO ❧

Borrow a coin and display it between your left thumb and forefinger (**1**). Perform the "Voodoo Coin Vanish" (**2**), apparently taking the coin away in your right fist, but actually retaining it in a left hand finger palm (**3**). Reach inside your jacket with your left hand (**4**) and secretly drop the coin down your sleeve opening. In the same action bring out the pen (**5**).

Practise until the movements are smooth and it looks as if you have merely reached into your pocket to bring out the pen (**6**).

Tap your right fist with the pen (**7**). Open the fist to show that your hand is completely empty – the coin has vanished (**8**)! Display your "magic pen" proudly and at the same time lower your right hand to your side, cupping the fingers (**9**). The coin that you placed in the top of your sleeve will now slide down and drop into your cupped fingers (**10**). Close your right hand into a fist again and tap it with the magic pen (**11**). Open your hand – the coin has magically reappeared (**12**)!

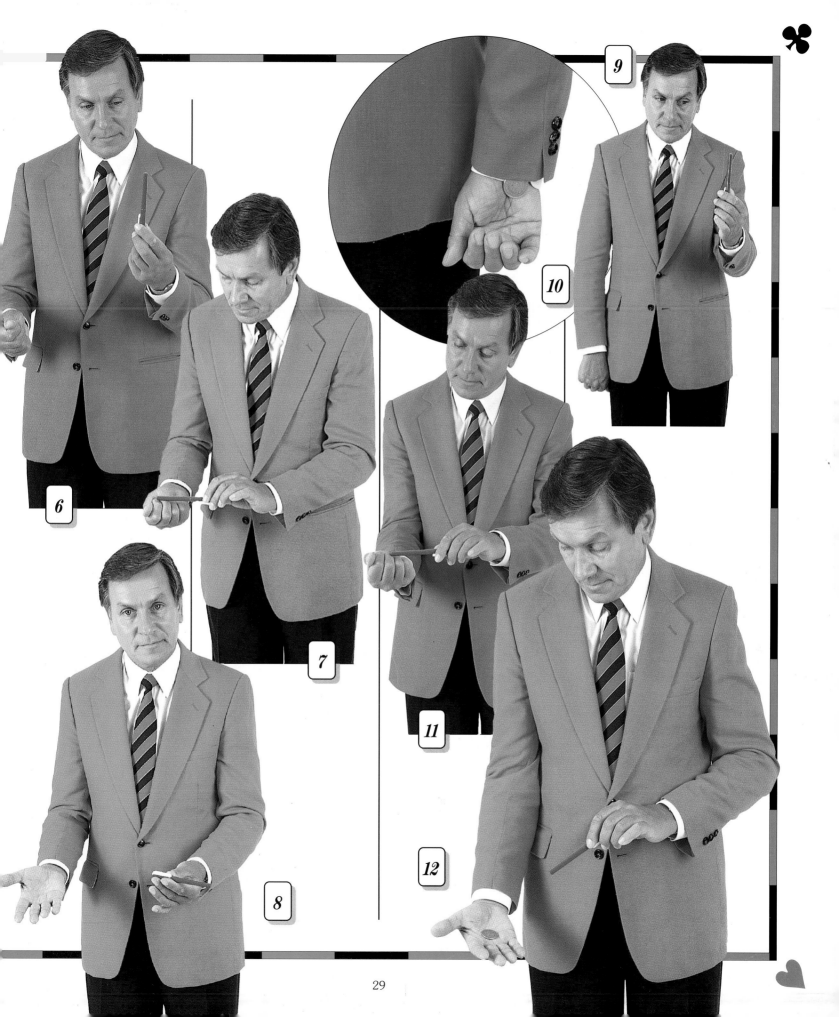

6

7

8

9

10

11

12

SNAPPY COIN TRICK

Coin tricks are always fun to do. This is probably the fastest one that I know. Be careful not to fool yourself.

◀ EFFECT ▶

You openly drop a coin into your sleeve and then magically pluck it through the cloth at your elbow.

REQUIREMENTS
Just a small coin
You must wear a jacket

vanishes (**2**). The reveal photograph (**3**) shows what actually happens. The bottom edge of the coin slides away across your thumb and the top edge drops and, as you grip it, it becomes hidden by the fleshy parts of your finger and thumb. You will soon get the hang of it. Once you feel confident that you can do the Snap Vanish, proceed as described.

Sit with your *right* side turned towards the spectators. Bend your left arm and rest your left elbow on the table. Hold the coin over the opening of your left sleeve (**4**) and perform the Snap Vanish. It will appear that you have dropped the coin down your sleeve (**5**).

Don't move your right hand.

◆ WHAT YOU DO ◆

First you must learn and practise the "Snap Vanish" of a coin. It is really an optical illusion – very easy to do – but most deceptive! Hold the coin between your right index finger and thumb (**1**). Force the finger and thumb together with a "snap". The coin apparently

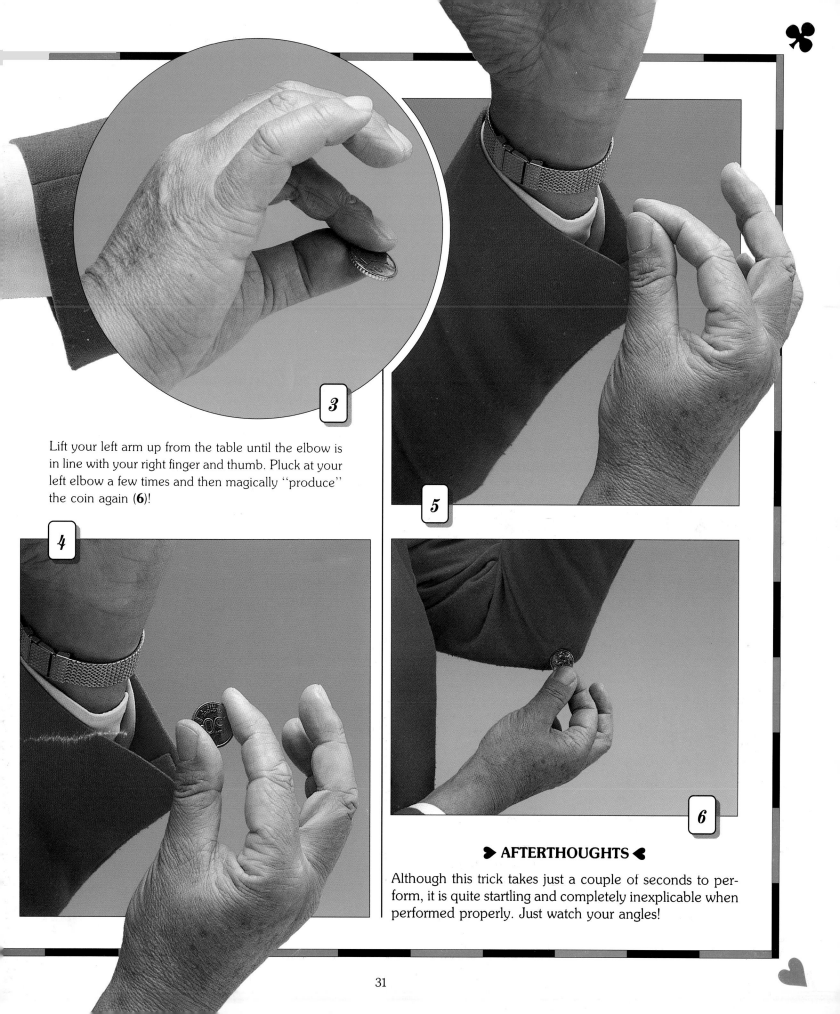

Lift your left arm up from the table until the elbow is in line with your right finger and thumb. Pluck at your left elbow a few times and then magically "produce" the coin again (**6**)!

3

5

4

6

> **AFTERTHOUGHTS** <

Although this trick takes just a couple of seconds to perform, it is quite startling and completely inexplicable when performed properly. Just watch your angles!

"GONE!"

This classic of close-up magic is as delightful to perform as it is to watch – a real object lesson in presentation, misdirection and timing.

◀ EFFECT ▶

A borrowed, marked coin is placed beneath an upturned glass. Not only does the coin vanish but the glass vanishes too!

REQUIREMENTS
A glass tumbler
A piece of A4-size paper or a good quality napkin
A small adhesive label
A pen
A large coin (which is borrowed)

♣ WHAT YOU DO ♣

Sit at a table with your legs tucked well under it. Borrow a large coin. Give the coin's owner the adhesive label and have him stick it on to his coin anyway that he wishes – front, back, even on its edge – it is up to him. Give him the pen and have him write his initials on the label. When he has done this (**1**), you turn the tumbler upside down (**2**) and fashion a paper cover around it with the paper (**3**). It should be folded loosely enough to slide easily off and yet firm enough to retain the shape of the glass (**4**).

"I'm going to show you a trick called 'Gone'."

Place the coin, marked side up, on the table about 30cm in front of you. Put the covered glass over it (**5**).

"Anything that I place under the glass will disappear when I say the magic word 'Go'. I just have to say 'Go' and the coin will disappear, because that's what happens when I say 'Go'. The coin vanishes. In a moment I will say 'Go' and it will be gone."

"Right, the coin will now disappear! 'Go'!"

Lift up the cover and tumbler together (**10**) and swing your hand inwards as before. Keep it low. As soon as it is over your lap area (**11**), ease your grip a little and let the glass drop silently into your lap (**12**). You keep hold of the paper cover which, of course, still retains the shape of the glass. Nobody will notice because they are all looking at the coin on the table, which *has not* vanished, and you have already acclimatized them to the to-ing and fro-ing of the glass and cover.

While you are spouting the above "garbage" you perform the following actions *at least three times*. With your right hand slide the paper cover about half-way up the tumbler showing the coin (**6**). Lower the cover again. Lift up the cover *and* glass together by gripping them firmly. Then swing your arm back so that the glass and cover are just hovering above the edge of the table – over your lap (**7**). Move your right hand forward again and replace the glass and cover back over the coin (**8**). These actions must accompany the "patter" and the combination of words and actions are designed to draw the onlookers' attention to the *coin*. To increase their attention on it, you can even turn it face-side down at one point in the routine (**9**). Why is this important? *Because we are now going to vanish the glass instead*!

"Oh dear! It didn't work. Perhaps it would be better turned over the other way. I'll try."

Turn over the coin (**13**) and put the *cover* back over it (**14**). The spectators will subconsciously assume that the tumbler is there too.

"O.K. I'm ready . . . 'Go'."

Lift the cover up to expose the coin again (**15**) but *do not swing it towards you this time*. Look at the coin with apparent dismay and desperation. Then, as if light was suddenly dawning, say:

"I'm sorry! I got a little confused. This is the trick where the *glass* vanishes!!!"

Open up the paper cover to show that the glass really has gone (**16**). The effect is astonishing! Crumple the paper cover up into a ball and throw it into the audience. This causes more mayhem. Take advantage of the uproar. Reach into your lap with your *left* hand. Grab the tumbler and push it up on the outside of your jacket. Grip it under your armpit (**17**). You must be very quick about this. Once it is safely in place, just *relax*. After a few seconds the spectators will turn back to you.

"If you look carefully you will see where the glass went."

Somebody will eventually spot it and point it out to the rest. Place it on the table with a flourish (**18**).

"This is the vanishing glass . . . and *this* . . ."

Reach forward with your right hand towards the coin (**19**), pulling it back towards you and execute the "Sitting-Down Coin Vanish" (**20**). Lean forward with your right fist closed (**21**), then slowly open your fingers (**22**) . . .

". . . is the vanishing coin . . . which has completely disappeared!"

➤ AFTERTHOUGHTS ◀

There is quite a lot to learn here. However, the sequences are all logical and easy to perform. Needless to say, you *must* practise until you can perform all the actions smoothly. Set a table up in front of a mirror. See what it looks like from the audience's point of view. Be careful not to fool yourself!

"MONEY TO BURN"

The humour in this next classic trick is derived from watching the reactions of your volunteer to the bizarre situation in which he finds himself. **Children should have adult supervision for this trick because of the use of matches! The ashtray should be used over a large noninflammable surface, such as a metal tray.**

♣ EFFECT ♣

You borrow the highest denomination banknote that you can persuade the spectator to part with. Having sealed it in an envelope, you proceed to set fire to it! Everything is reduced to ashes! You resurrect it from the ashes in a most amusing way and return it to the relieved spectator.

REQUIREMENTS
A borrowed banknote
A standard letter envelope
Box of matches and ashtray
A pack of cards
A pen or pencil

◆ PREPARATION ◆

Cut a 4cm slit in the envelope on the *address* side (**1**). If the envelope is shown flap side up, the slit should be hidden from view by the back pouch. Set up by putting the envelope and the pencil in your inside jacket pocket. Put the matches and the pack of cards in your left jacket pocket. We will call the idiot (sorry, volunteer!) who lends you the money Neil.

◀ WHAT YOU DO ▶

Talk to Neil:

"Lend me a banknote, Neil, and I will show you a fantastic trick!"

Neil obliges and lends you a note. You might be lucky and get a really high-value note; gratefully accept whatever he offers you. Take the pencil out of your pocket and hand it to Neil.

"In case you are fortunate enough to see your money again, I would like you to sign your name across it."

While he does this you remove the envelope from your pocket and place it (address side down) on the table.

"Did you know that paper money is virtually indestructible? Let me show you . . ."

Take the signed note from Neil (**2**) and fold it in half *three times* so that you end up with a little packet

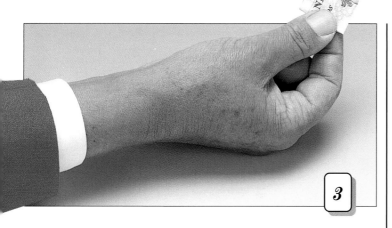

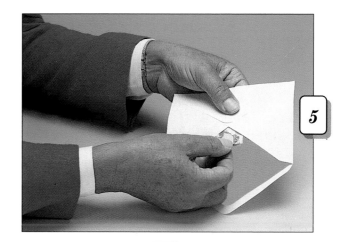

approximately 4cm square (**3**). Put the folded note on the table. Hold the envelope in your left hand, fingers covering the secret slit, thumb on top (**4**). Pull back the flap with your right hand, pick up the note and push it into the envelope (**5**). The leading edge of the folded note goes through the slit on to the *outside* of the envelope (**6**) and is hidden by your left fingers. Neil can still see part of his note on the inside of the envelope.

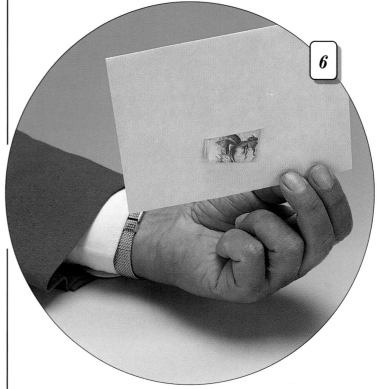

Lift the flap up to your mouth by raising your left hand, and lick the sticky flap. Lower your hand again so that Neil gets one last flash of his money, then fold the flap over and press it down to seal the envelope (**7**). Your right hand takes the envelope away and places it on the table. *At the same time* your left fingers hang on to his folded note and, without hesitation, you thrust your hand into your left jacket pocket. When your left hand is out of sight, push the folded note into the middle of the pack of cards.

Leave it there and bring out the box of matches. Your two hands have moved in opposite directions simultaneously. The actions are very natural and because of this will not cause suspicion. Practise until you can synchronize the two actions smoothly.

"You will enjoy this Neil! I'm going to set fire to your money! Please don't worry about it – I've done this trick before! Once!"

the secret slit area – thus you destroy the evidence (**9**)! You must now give an Oscar-winning performance . . . Smilingly you say:

"The amazing thing, Neil, is that your money will have withstood the heat and flames and will be completely unharmed! Let me show you . . ."

Pull the ashtray towards you. Strike a match and then, holding the envelope by one corner, apply the flame to the diagonally opposite corner (**8**). Be careful; don't burn your fingers! Just make sure that you destroy as much of the envelope as possible – especially

Start to poke about amongst the ashes looking for his money (**10**). Slowly your smile and confident attitude change to embarrassment and an air of doom.

"Oh dear!" You look shocked. Poke about some more (**11**). **"It seems to have gone slightly wrong. I just can't understand it. It worked fine last time . . ."** You give up your forlorn search for his money. **"Look, Neil, I'm terribly sorry . . . Let me show you a card trick instead!"**

Bring the pack out of your pocket and place it face downwards on the table. The note, you will remember, is sandwiched in the middle of the pack.

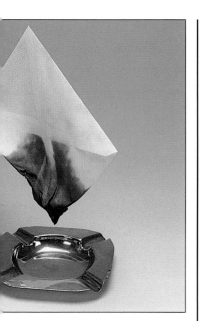

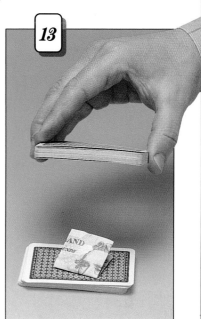

"I want you to cut the pack somewhere near the middle."

He will automatically lift off all the cards above the folded note (**12**), bringing it into view in a surprising way (**13**).

"Oh! Now I remember how to do the trick! Pick up the note, Neil. Open it up. Check your signature. Is that your note? The one that we burned?"

Neil will breathe a sigh of relief at getting his money back (**14**). You can now remind him that it is his turn to buy the drinks!

PART TWO

SAFETY PIN MAGIC

WARNING:
To avoid injury, children should have
adult supervision for the following tricks,
which use safety pins!

SPOOKY PINS

Tricks that use ordinary household objects are always effective because the spectators can "relate" to them easily. Our association with safety pins often began on the day that we wore our first nappy!

♣ EFFECT ♣

Two perfectly ordinary safety pins are firmly linked together. You hold one in each hand and pull in opposite directions. They become magically unlinked without opening!

◆ WHAT YOU DO ◆

The trick is self-working provided that you link and hold the pins exactly as shown (**1**). Note particularly the position of the *opening* and *non-opening* bars of the two safety pins (**2**). Once you are sure that you have the correct position, hold them firmly and pull your hands *sharply* in opposite directions. The pins will separate automatically (**3**). Practise until you can unlink them smoothly. It is a little knack that you will very soon acquire.

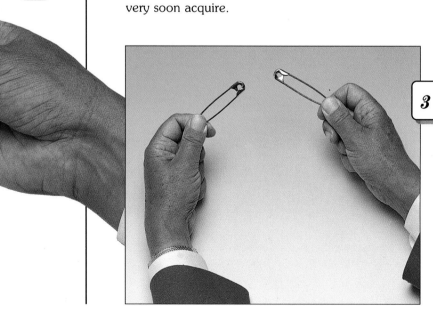

HANKY PANKY

Another little safety pin gem. It looks quite impossible, while, in fact, it is entirely self-working.

➤ EFFECT ◄

A safety pin is fastened to a handkerchief. You remove it without opening it!

REQUIREMENTS
One good-sized safety pin
A linen handkerchief, which is best borrowed

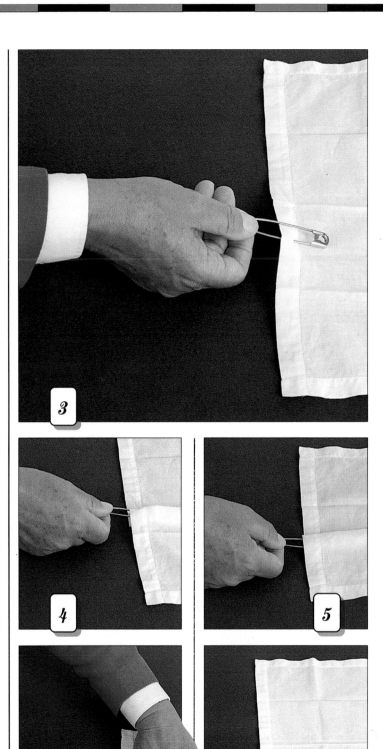

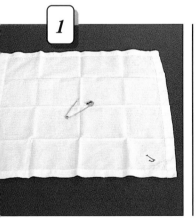

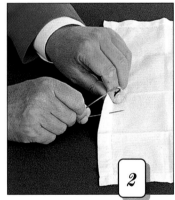

◄ WHAT YOU DO ➤

Follow the instructions and you will find the trick self-working. Spread the handkerchief out on the table (**1**). Fasten the safety pin on to the handkerchief near its edge (**2**). Turn the pin over to the left – *three times*. The handkerchief will, of course, roll over too (**3**, **4**, **5**). Press firmly down on the handkerchief with your left hand to hold it firmly in place. Grip the protruding end of the pin between your right forefinger and thumb and *pull down sharply*. The pin comes off cleanly and yet is still closed (**6**)! Return the un-damaged handkerchief (**7**) to the amazed spectator.

A RIPPING YARN!

Don't do this trick in front of people of a nervous disposition! It is hard on their nerves!

♣ EFFECT ♣

A spectator holds up her handkerchief before her. You fasten a safety pin in the hem at one end, give it a sharp pull and the pin ends up at the *other* end, still fastened! Although a resounding ripping sound is heard, the handkerchief remains undamaged.

REQUIREMENTS
A good-sized safety pin
A linen handkerchief, borrowed if possible

◆ WHAT YOU DO ◆

The spectator should hold the handkerchief tautly as shown in picture (**1**). You should insert the safety pin at the point in the hem shown (**2**). Note that the solid (non-opening) bar of the pin is to your *left* (**3**). *This is very important.* Grip the end of the pin firmly (**4**) and pull the pin sharply to the *right* (**5**) for about 20cm (**6**) and then push in. The pin will still be fastened but is

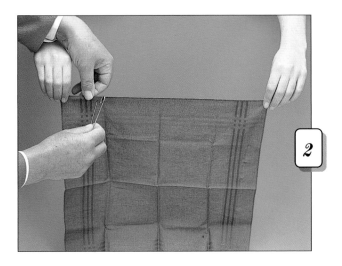

now at the other end of the handkerchief. And despite the sound of tearing, the handkerchief will be intact (**7**).

I suggest that you try this on your own handkerchief until you get the hang of it. It is an easily acquired knack. Picture (**5**) shows what happens when you pull the pin to the right. The bar disengages slightly from the clasp, allowing the point of the pin to slide along the cloth without damaging it. You must push in at the end of your "run" to make the pin penetrate the handkerchief again, and so complete the illusion.

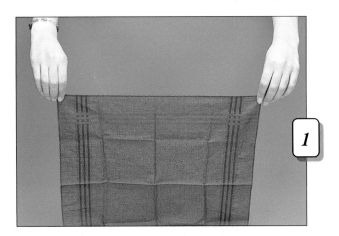

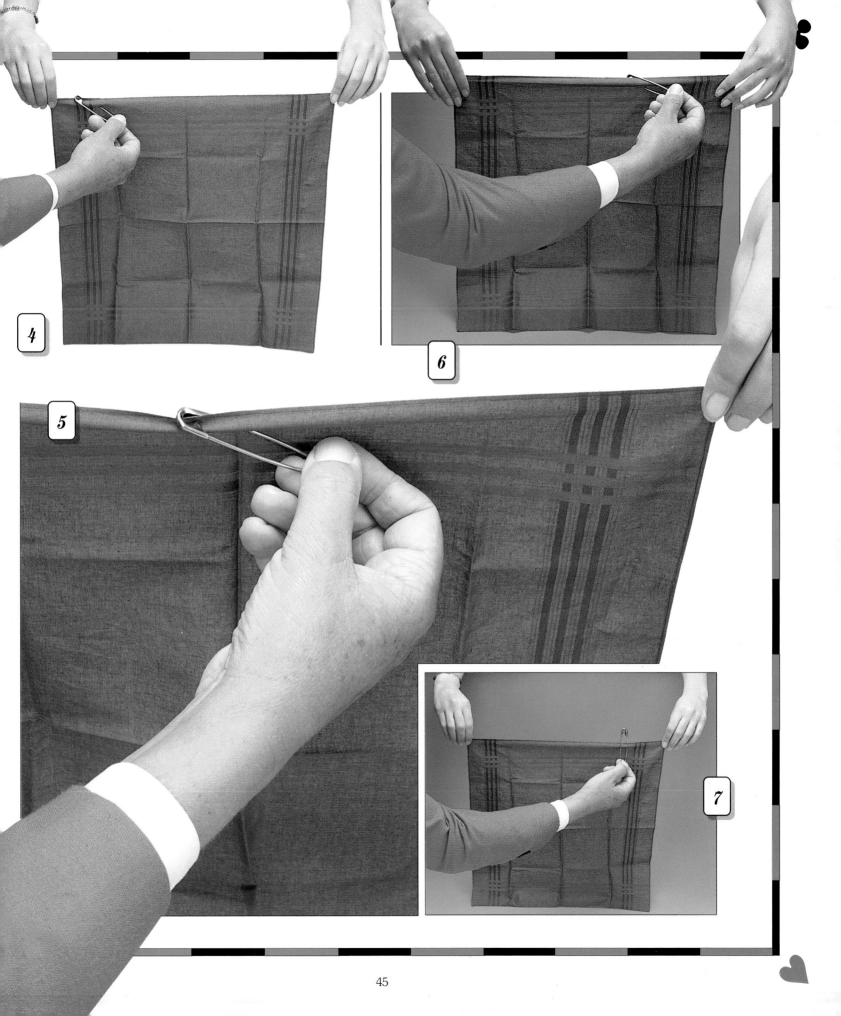

DROP OUT

This unusual "quick trick" is really an optical illusion. It should fool most people.

♣ EFFECT ♣

Two *closed* safety pins are shown. You just drop them gently on to the table and both spring open as if by magic!

← PREPARATION →

The pins are *never* closed! Look at picture (**1**) carefully. It shows two opened safety pins with their *pins* resting in each other's *shields*. If you now hold the safety pins with your thumb covering the loops (**2**) it will appear that you are holding two closed safety pins! The illusion is perfect.

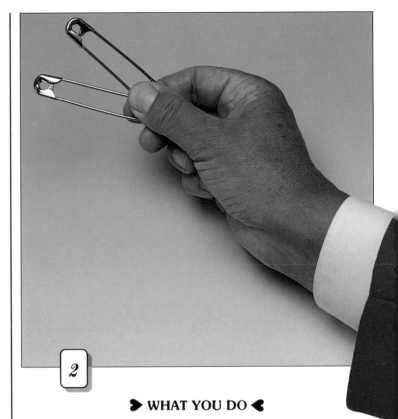

➤ WHAT YOU DO ◄

Display the two safety pins in your hand as shown (**2**). Point out to the spectator that they are securely fastened. Hold them about 30cm above the centre of your table. Drop the safety pins. They will naturally come to rest in the open position (**3**). Now close each safety pin properly and give them to the spectator to try and duplicate your feat!

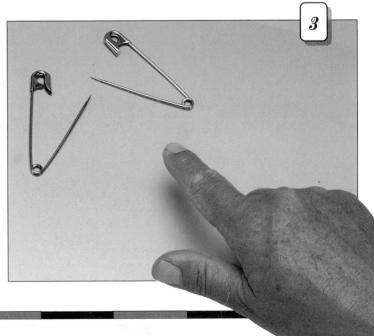

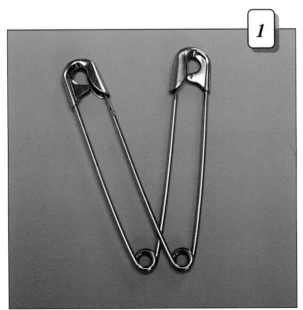

PIN IN A SPIN

This mini-miracle is a superb optical illusion. It will baffle even the most eagle-eyed of spectators.

◆ EFFECT ◆

A matchstick repeatedly penetrates through the bar of a safety pin.

REQUIREMENTS
A safety pin
A matchstick

First cut off the head of the matchstick so that both ends look the same (**1**). Then carefully impale this matchstick on the safety pin (**2**). Make sure that the safety pin passes through the centre of the matchstick. At first you may find that the matchstick splits. Try again until you find one that does not. Twist the matchstick backwards and forwards until it revolves easily and freely on the bar.

◄ WHAT YOU DO ►

Hold the pin between your left finger and thumb (**3**). Make sure that the matchstick is impaled by the bar *nearest* you and rests under the bar *furthest* away from you.

To create the illusion that the matchstick penetrates the solid bar of the safety pin, just flick down sharply on the end nearest to you (**4**). The far end of the match (B) will appear to penetrate the bar that it was resting under. It is now seen to be on the upperside of the bar (**5**)! What actually happens is this: if you flick hard enough, the matchstick will rebound and spin round in the opposite direction. It is really end "A" that now rests on the bar and *not* end "B"! The matchstick has turned full circle but too quickly to be followed by the naked eye.

You will have to try this out in your own hands to appreciate the effect. It is very deceptive and can be repeated as often as you wish.

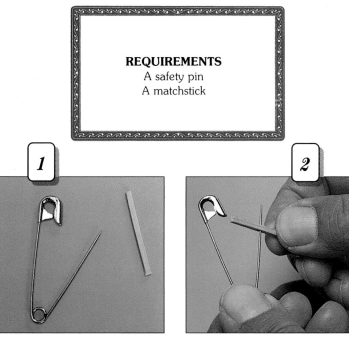

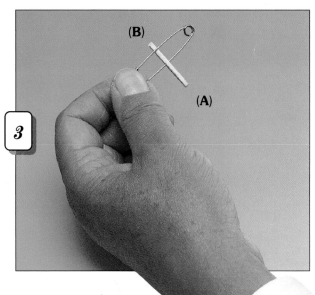

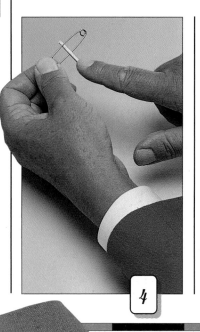

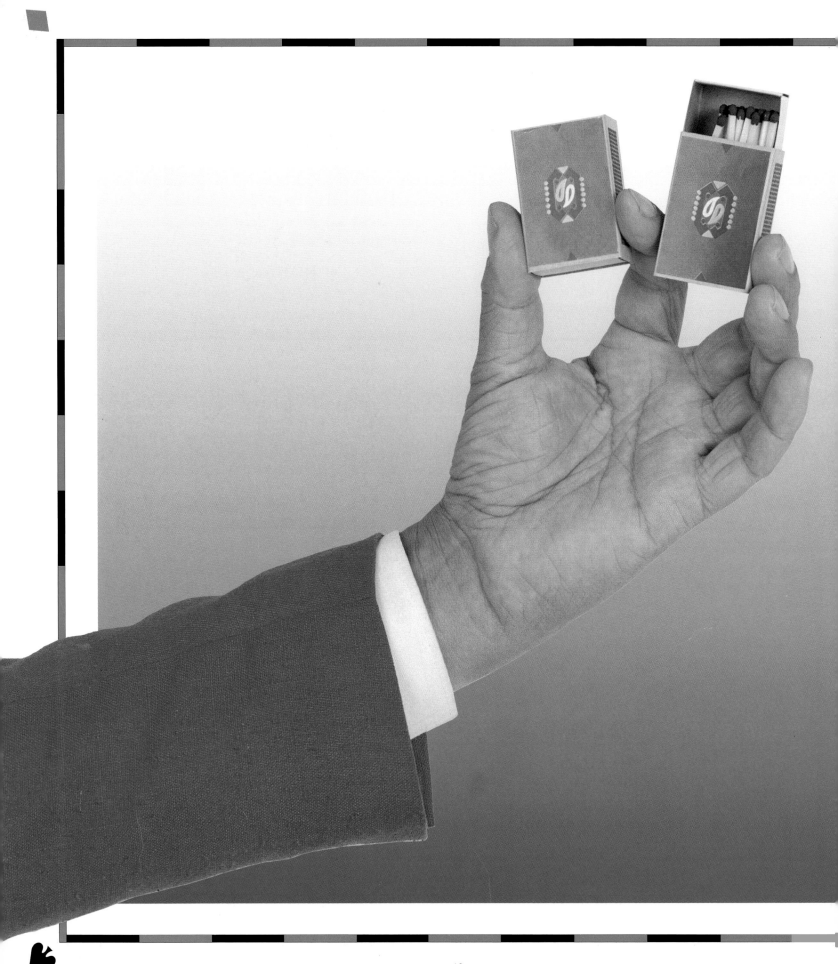

PART THREE

MATCHBOX MAGIC

SOUNDS EASY

Tricks that rely on *sound* are very rare in magic. This is a good one and the method employed is very subtle.

♣ EFFECT ♣

Three empty matchboxes are shown and a borrowed coin dropped into one of them. The spectator is asked to remember which matchbox the coin is in. Slowly and deliberately you mix the boxes around. No matter how carefully she looks, the spectator is never able to pick out the correct box! Finally the coin completely disappears and is produced from your jacket pocket!

REQUIREMENTS
Four identical empty matchboxes

Two coins (one of which must be borrowed)
Elastic band
Small sticky labels
A pen
A spectator. We will call her Louise.

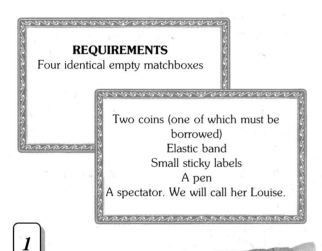

1

◆ PREPARATION ◆

Put *your* coin in a matchbox and strap it to the underside of your left wrist. It should rest just out of sight up your jacket sleeve (**1**). If you now shake your left hand you will hear a rattling sound. Put the three empty matchboxes in your right jacket pocket with the labels and the pen. You are all set.

➤ WHAT YOU DO ◀

Start by saying:

"Lend me a coin, Louise, and I will show you a famous circus trick."

Louise lends you the coin although she secretly wonders if she will *ever* see it again! Bring out the pen, sticky labels and one matchbox. Have the coin labelled and marked as in previous tricks (**2**). Remove the drawer from the matchbox to show that it is empty. Place the marked coin in the matchbox and shut the drawer (**3**). You are now going secretly to remove her coin from the box.

Hold the box upside down in the rattling position (**4**) and give the sides a little squeeze (**5**). The coin will slide out on to your palm (**6**). Place the box on the table keeping the coin palmed in your right hand. This move should be practised until you can do it smoothly. It should seem that you merely rattled the box, then placed it on the table.

Now put your hand in your pocket – leave the coin there – bring out the other two empty matchboxes. Show these to be absolutely empty, reassemble them and place them on the table to the *right* of the other one (**7**).

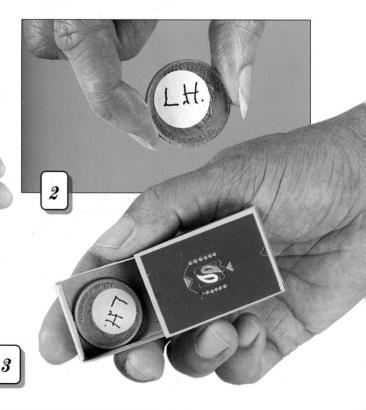

2

3

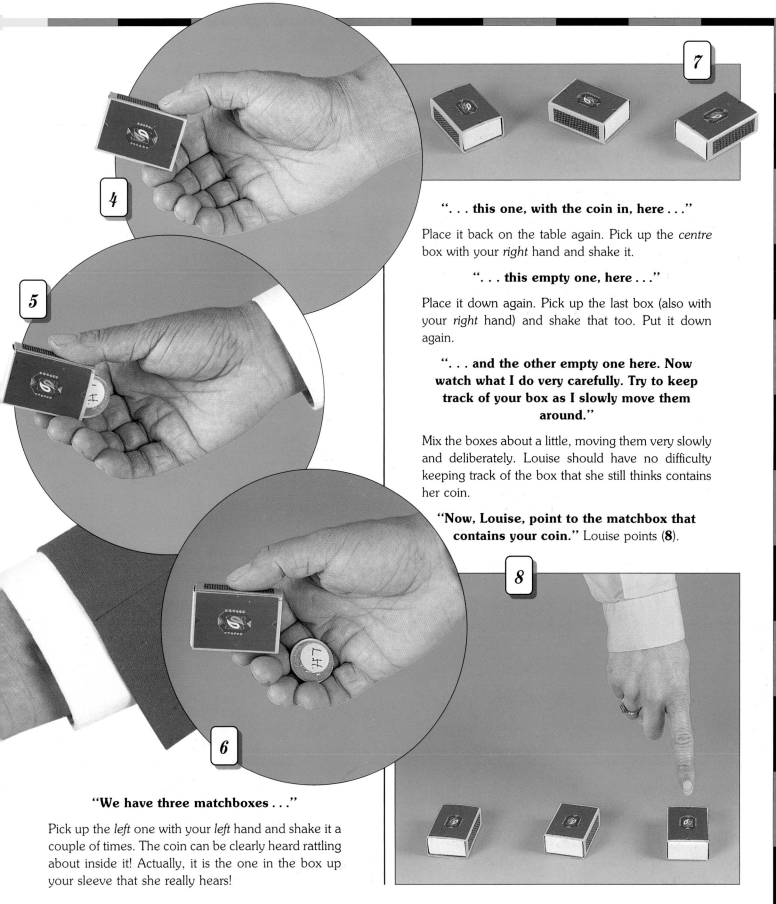

4

7

"... this one, with the coin in, here ..."

Place it back on the table again. Pick up the *centre* box with your *right* hand and shake it.

"... this empty one, here ..."

Place it down again. Pick up the last box (also with your *right* hand) and shake that too. Put it down again.

"... and the other empty one here. Now watch what I do very carefully. Try to keep track of your box as I slowly move them around."

Mix the boxes about a little, moving them very slowly and deliberately. Louise should have no difficulty keeping track of the box that she still thinks contains her coin.

"Now, Louise, point to the matchbox that contains your coin." Louise points (**8**).

5

8

6

"We have three matchboxes ..."

Pick up the *left* one with your *left* hand and shake it a couple of times. The coin can be clearly heard rattling about inside it! Actually, it is the one in the box up your sleeve that she really hears!

We will let her win the first round! Pick up the one that she indicates with your *left* hand and shake it (**9**). It rattles – so this time she is correct. Shuffle the boxes around on the table again. Ask Louise to point again (**10**). Notice that we always say *"point"* and not *"choose"*. That is because we do not want Louise to pick up the box that she selects. This time pick up the selected box with your *right* hand and shake it (**11**). It will not rattle. Pick up one of the other boxes with your *left* hand and shake it (**12**).

"No Louise. I caught you that time. *This* is the one – over here!"

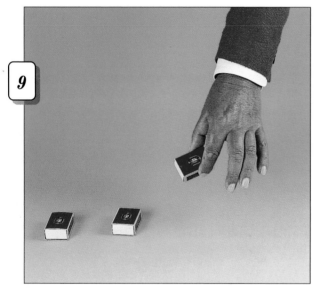

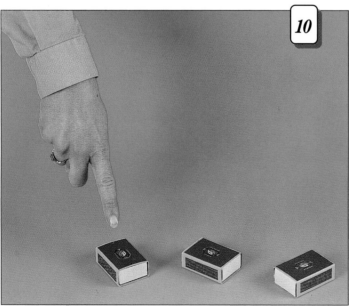

Place the box that apparently contains the coin between the other two and slowly mix them around again. Louise points to a box once more. Again prove that she is wrong by shaking her selected box with your *right* hand and one of the others with your *left*! By this time Louise will be thinking of having her *eyes* tested at the earliest opportunity!

Now we "kick her when she is down". Place the box that she thinks contains the coin a little apart from the other two. Give it a shake with your left hand so that she can hear the "rattle". Gesture with both your hands to show that they are empty as you say:

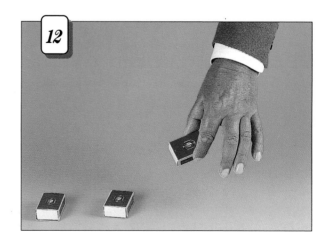

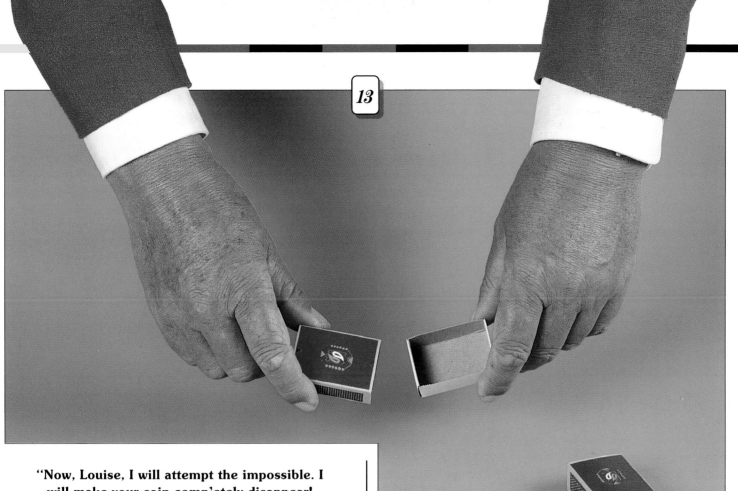

13

"Now, Louise, I will attempt the impossible. I will make your coin completely disappear! Watch!"

Wave your right hand mysteriously over the box and then count . . .

"One . . . Two . . . Three! Now I shall open the box."

You open the box and show that the coin has gone (**13**). Louise will immediately grab for the other two boxes in a vain search for her coin. Too late! Bring the trick to a stunning conclusion by producing the marked coin from your pocket (**14**).

❦ AFTERTHOUGHTS ❧

On occasions I have been able secretly to slip the spectator's coin into *her own jacket pocket*! The mixing about of the boxes provides the misdirection that makes this possible. The trick then becomes a little miracle because you state that you will make the coin jump from the matchbox into her own pocket! You then ask Louise to produce her marked coin herself! The *effect* is stunning! If you think that you can get away with it, without spoiling the trick, then *go for it*! He who dares – wins!

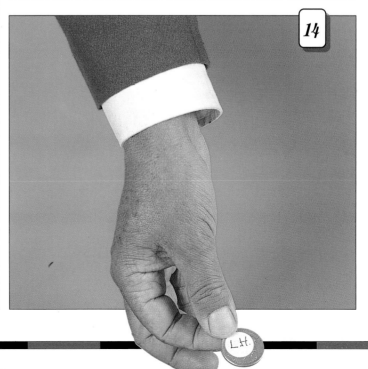

14

THE ACROBATIC MATCHBOX

This little gem has been my favourite "pocket trick" for more than 35 years. I pass the routine on to you with pride and the wish that you practise it until you can perform it perfectly. Do not be put off because the effect is achieved by using a secret thread. If you perform it correctly, *no one will ever know*!

❖ EFFECT ❖

A matchbox is placed on the back of your hand. It suddenly "comes to life" and performs some staggering acrobatic feats. It stands up on its end. The drawer suddenly rises. It then runs down your wrist, does a twirl and stands on its side. For a finale, it does a complete somersault, stands up and then opens all by itself! In explanation, you state that this is all made possible by using an invisible hair. You pretend to pluck a hair from a spectator's head and attach it to an invisible hook on the end of the matchbox. When you "pull" the hair, the drawer of the matchbox is seen to open as if being pulled by the hair!

REQUIREMENTS
A matchbox
A length of thin nylon fishing line or
dressmaker's invisible thread
A small safety pin
A needle

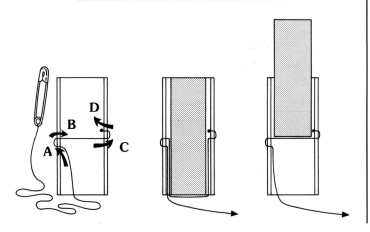

❯ PREPARATION ❮

You will have to "gimmick up" the matchbox. *N.B.* I have used black thread in the photographs, so that you can see how the tricks work. For performance you should use colourless fishing line. First make sure that the drawer slides in and out smoothly and does not jam. Thread about 50cm of nylon fishing line on to your needle. Now thread it through the matchbox as shown in the diagram. First remove the drawer. Then, from the inside, push the needle through the outer cover so that it comes out on the outside of the box about half way up (**A**). Move the needle up about 5mm, and thread it back through the box again (**B**), across, and out through the middle of the other side (**C**). Go up another 5mm and push the needle through again from the outside (**D**), only this time do not thread it right across – just pass the needle up through the sleeve and out at the top. Remove the needle and tie about three knots in the end of the thread, all on top of one another. This knot will now be too fat to unthread through the holes in the matchbox case.

Put the drawer back in the case from the top. It will take up some of the slack thread. Place a light pencil dot on the underside of the box at the end furthest from where the thread runs under the drawer. This will not be noticed by the spectators. It is there so that you can tell at a glance which side is which. Tie a safety pin on the other end of the thread. Fasten the safety pin to the inside of your left jacket pocket and after putting a few matches in the box, place it in the same pocket. Your simple preparation having been completed, you are now ready to perform.

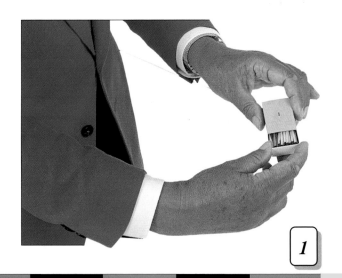

◆ WHAT YOU DO ◆

Take the box out with your left hand and hold it by its long edges about half way along. Your right hand comes over and holds the box by its free end, between your right thumb and index finger. Push open the drawer with your left thumb and remove it completely between your right index finger and thumb in the usual manner (**1**). The fingers of your *left* hand retain hold of the cover, and the thread is completely hidden by your left hand and coat sleeve. Both hands should be held across the body and the two sections of the box displayed by moving your wrists, *not* your arms. Be content to show the box for a second very casually but not carelessly, and then assemble the box as before.

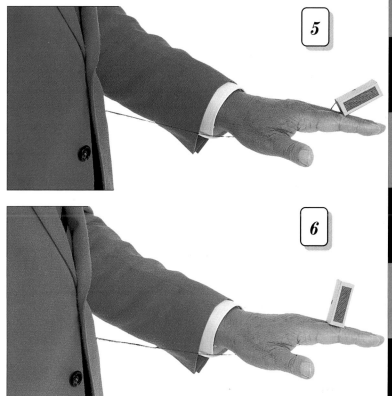

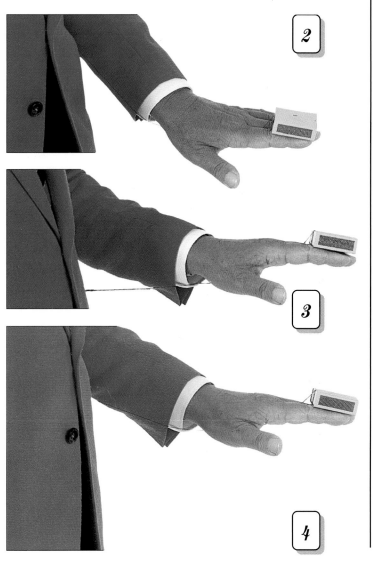

The box should now be held in your left hand between your index finger and thumb. Take the box in you right hand (index finger and thumb) straighten the fingers of your left hand and, holding this hand in a horizontal position, place the matchbox on the back of this hand with the pencil dot uppermost and nearest the finger-tips (**2**). The thread must be arranged so that it passes from the top of the end nearest your body, between the first and second fingers; under the palm and thence to your jacket pocket (**3**). You will discover that this is easily accomplished during the action of placing the box on the back of your hand. When the right fingers take the box, slightly part the first and second fingers of your left hand. By dropping this hand a little, you will engage the thread and it will pass between the required fingers. Then place the box on the hand as described. The end of the box nearest you should be resting on or near the middle joints of the fingers (**4**). *This is very important*.

If, with the box still on the back of your hand, you push your hand *gently* forward a little, you will find that the box will be levered up into a standing position (**5, 6**). This is caused by the pull on the thread originating from the forward movement of the hand.

By pushing your hand still further forward, you will find that the drawer will rise up from its cover (**7**). If this does not happen, it means that your thread is too long and you will have to shorten it. The thread will be of the correct length if, when you stand with your hand and arm held at waist level with the box as in picture (**4**), there is no slackness in the thread. Check also that your pencil dot is uppermost.

The big drawback with moving your hand forward in this way is that a fairly observant spectator may notice it. I have only described it in order that you may readily grasp the working principle of the matchbox. I work my matchbox by moving my body and not my hand. This is by far the best method because the hand stays motionless throughout the routine. This pretty routine is in six parts and we are now ready to start.

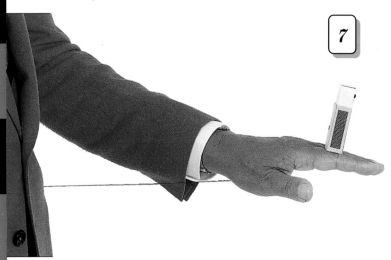

➤ EFFECT NO 1 ◄

Place the box on the back of your left hand, as shown in picture (**4**). Keep your hand stationary but bend your body at the waist, apparently bowing over the box. At the same time give a waving gesture, simulating a magic pass, with the free right hand. These are perfectly natural actions but necessary from our point of view. You will find that the slight bending movement of the body will bring pull to bear on the thread and the box will lever itself into a standing position (**5, 6**). By bending the body a little more or, alternatively, pulling your left side backwards a little, you will find that the drawer of the box will slowly rise (**7**).

Remember to keep the hand motionless.

◆ EFFECT NO 2 ◆

Close the box and place it, once again, on the back of your left hand. With your right hand slide the box straight back over your left hand until the end nearest you rests on, or very near, your wrist (**8**). The thread, as the photograph shows, now runs beneath the box, along the back of the hand, between the first and second fingers, under your hand, and thence to your pocket. Although about 4 or 5cm of thread is actually running across the back of your hand it will *never* be noticed. It is only on view for a second in any case, and the spectator does not have time to focus his eyes on it.

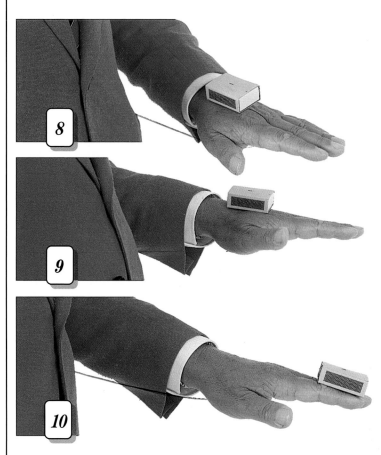

You will find now that by creating tension on the thread (i.e. by bending your body), the box will slowly crawl along the back of your hand (**9**) and finally come to rest at your finger tips (**10**). By pointing your fingers in a *slightly* downward direction, this movement of the box can be assisted. This matchbox move, like all the others, should be executed slowly and gracefully, avoiding all jerky actions.

♣ EFFECT NO 3 ♣

For this effect, turn the box so that the end where the thread makes its entry is *facing* the spectators (i.e. the pencil dot is nearest to you) and place the box at the extreme tips of the *second and third* fingers (**11**). Hold your hand perfectly relaxed and you will find that by bringing a slight but steady pressure to bear on the thread, the box will swing right round to occupy its former position (**12**), stand on end (**13, 14**), and finally raise its own drawer (**15**)! You will find it easier to perform the "swing round" movement if, once again, you point your fingers in a *slightly* downward direction. Remember, only slightly downwards – do not try to defy the law of gravity!

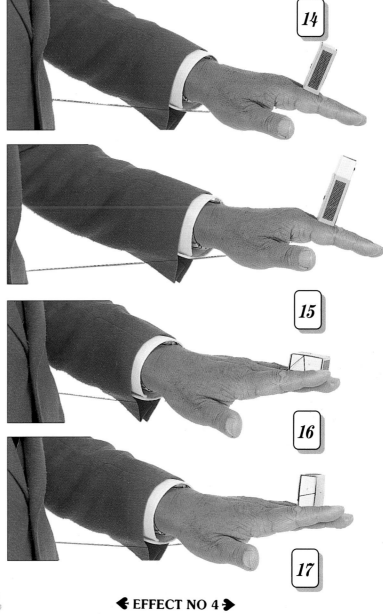

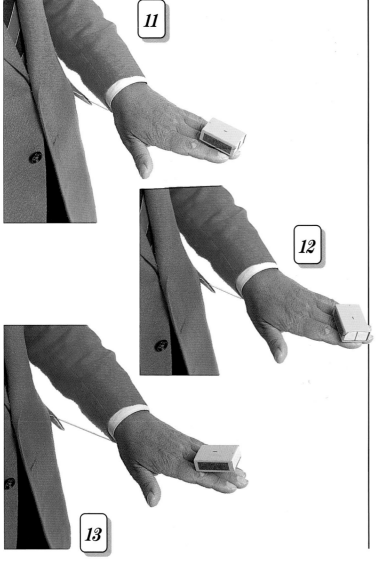

◀ EFFECT NO 4 ▶

Close the box and place it sideways across your second, third and fourth fingers, with the long edge resting on the far side of the middle joints. Raise your index finger very slightly until it rests alongside, but does not grip, the end of the box (**16**). Pulling on the thread now will cause the box to lever itself into an upright position standing on its *long edge* (**17**)! The position of the index finger is important because it prevents the box from pivoting round. The rough bumpy skin of the middle joints of the fingers also helps to keep the box crosswise on your hand, and so makes this effect possible.

♣ EFFECT NO 5 ♣

Now place the box on the back of your hand as in picture (**4**) once again. Pick up the box in your right hand by its near (attached) end: Draw the box towards yourself (**18**) and at the same time turn the box completely over (**19**) and lay it back on your hand again, quite close to your wrist (**20**). In this position the attached end of the box is towards the audience and a single strand of thread runs along the top of the box, down between your first and second fingers and thence to your pocket. If you bend the body again to pull the thread, the box will run down your hand (**21, 22**), turn a complete somersault (**23, 24, 25**), run down your hand again towards your fingertips (**26**), stand up on end (**27, 28**) and, finally, raise its own drawer once more (**29**)!

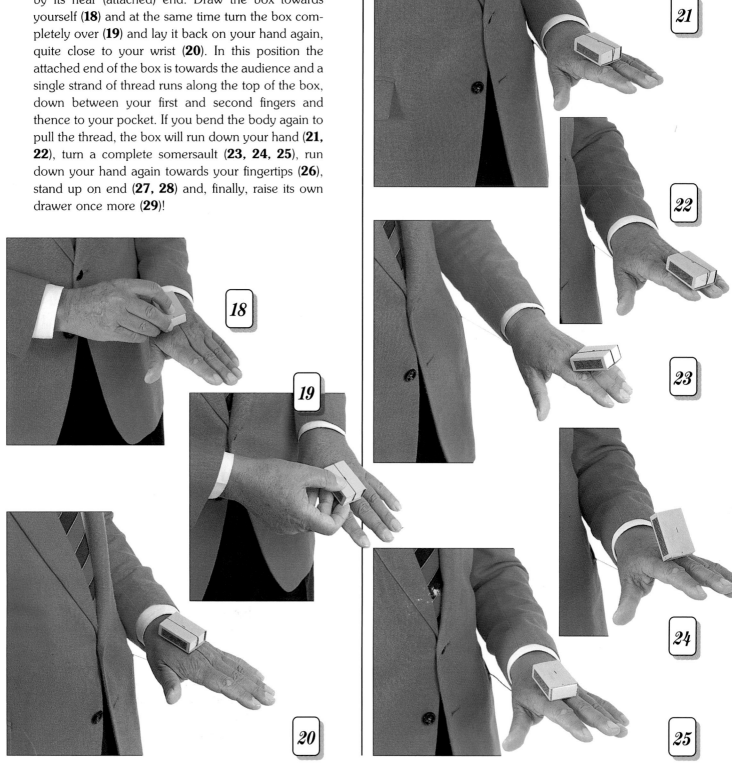

58

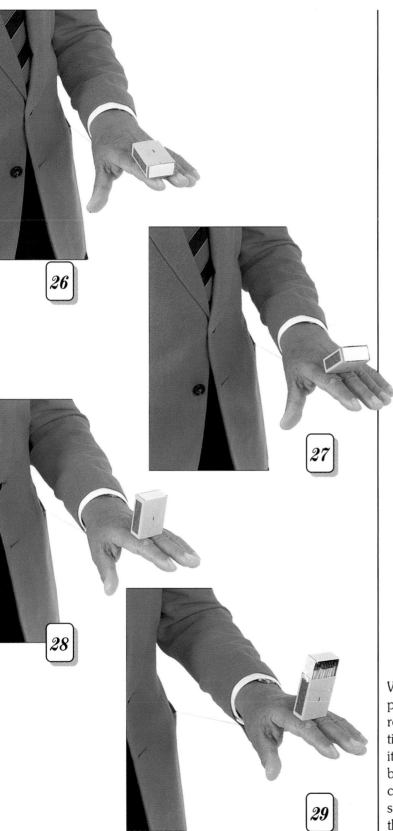

26

27

28

29

➤ EFFECT NO 6 ◀

Finally the box is reassembled and held by the left index finger and thumb as before. Tell your audience that, "The trick is made possible by using a hair". So saying, you pluck an *imaginary hair* from the head of a nearby spectator and wind the imaginary hair around an *imaginary hook* at the unattached end of the box. Pretend to pull on the end of this imaginary hair and, at the same time, bend your body to bring pressure to bear on the thread. This will cause the drawer to open (**30**). When these two actions are properly synchronized it will appear that the drawer of the matchbox is actually being pulled open by an invisible hair!

You have finished the sequence of six effects so turn your left side slightly, but not furtively, away from the audience and casually replace the matchbox into your left jacket pocket.

30

◀ AFTERTHOUGHTS ➤

Well, that's it! I have gone into great detail with the explanation so that you will be able to master the whole routine. You do not always have to perform it in its entirety. Practise with the first effect until you have mastered it – then have fun learning the other gymnastics! Remember, you should, of course, use nylon fishing line, which is colourless. It does not show up very well in photographs, so we have gimmicked our matchbox with *black cotton* for the sake of clarity.

THE WALKING DEAD

This is a wonderfully impossible looking trick that uses just a book of paper matches. The final effect really packs a punch! **Children should have adult supervision for this trick because of the use of matches!**

➤ EFFECT ◄

You let a spectator count the matches in a book of paper matches. Let us say there are thirteen. You tear out one match – strike it – then extinguish the flame. The match then *disappears*! The spectator recounts the matches in the book. There are *still* thirteen matches in the book even though you tore one out just a few seconds ago! To make matters worse, on closer inspection the spectator discovers that one of the matches is *dead – yet still firmly attached to the book*! Who said that the dead do not walk?!

REQUIREMENTS
Just a book of paper matches

◆ PREPARATION ◆

Bend back one match, light it and then quickly blow it out (**1**). Close the flap of the book and, in so doing, slide it between the spent match and the rest (**2**). Put the book away in your left pocket and you are ready to begin.

◄ WHAT YOU DO ➤

Remove the book of matches from your pocket. Before you actually bring it into view, fold back the spent match and cover it with your thumb (**3**). Open the flap with your right hand (**4**), and, still maintaining your left hand grip, ask the spectator to count how many matches there are in the book. He says "Thirteen".

"You counted them very well. Education is a wonderful thing – you must have gone to a *private* school!"

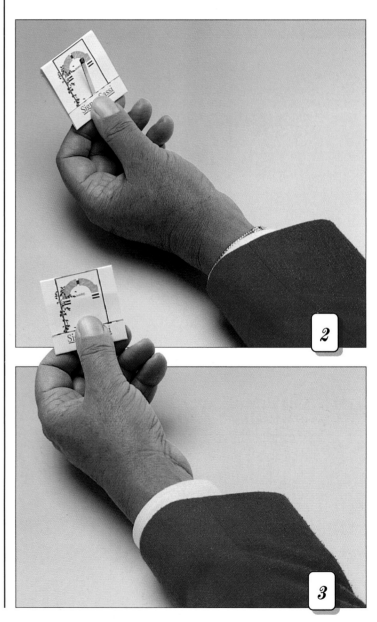

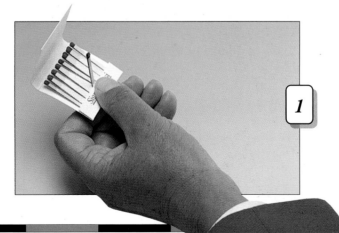

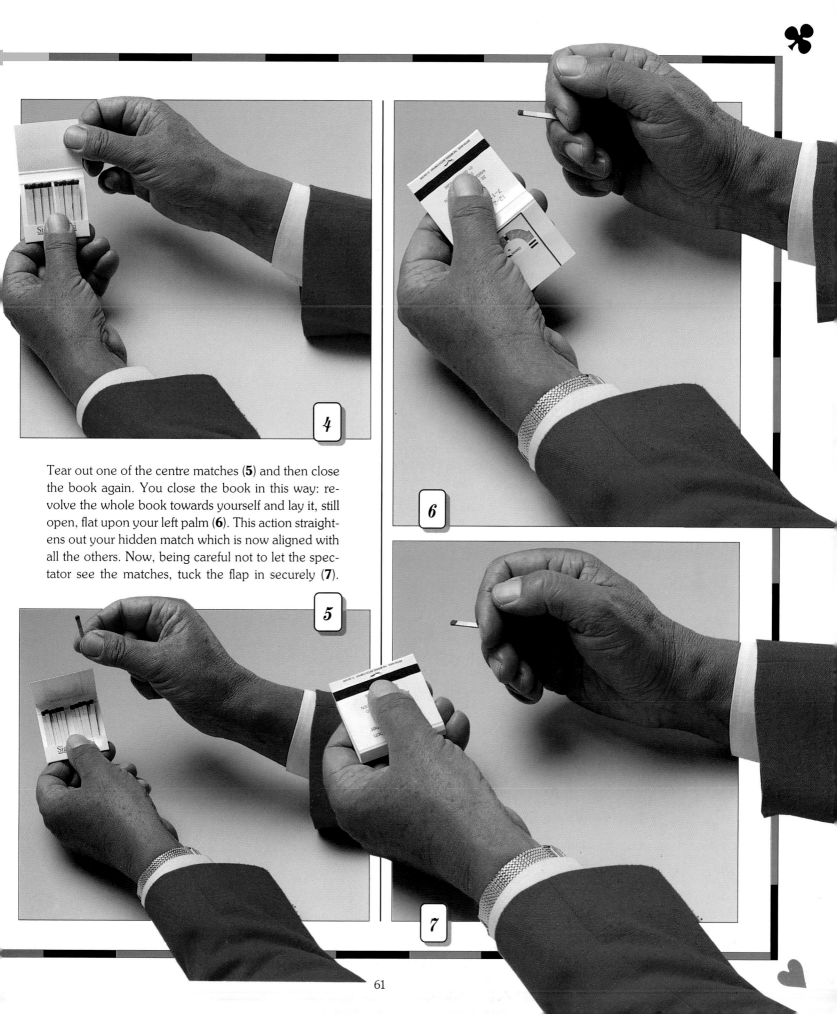

Tear out one of the centre matches (**5**) and then close the book again. You close the book in this way: revolve the whole book towards yourself and lay it, still open, flat upon your left palm (**6**). This action straightens out your hidden match which is now aligned with all the others. Now, being careful not to let the spectator see the matches, tuck the flap in securely (**7**).

Strike the match that you have torn out on the striking plate (**8**). As it starts to burn (**9**), put the book down on the table or bar.

Shake out the flame after a couple of seconds. This is the moment that you vanish the match! It will take a bit of practice but it is quite *easy* really. Just get your *timing* right. Shake the match diagonally upwards (**10**) and downwards across your body (**11**). On about the second or third shake the flame should go out. Keep shaking and on the downward stroke of about the fifth or sixth shake *let the match go*! Continue shaking as if you were still holding the match. Do not look down – look *up* throughout. Fix your *eyes* on the spot where your hand ends up when it reaches the top of its upswing.

If you are seated at a table when you perform this trick, the match will end up harmlessly in your lap. If you are standing at a bar, the match will end up on the floor somewhere. Either way it will not be noticed! Cheeky, isn't it! Methods in magic are really immaterial – it is the overall effect that counts. If the effect is the same, but there is an easy and a difficult way to achieve it, then it is only common sense to take the easy way out! Just *practise* until you can vanish the match smoothly.

Stop shaking your hand and look at your hand in amazement – the match has disappeared (**12**)! Where has it gone? Maybe it has gone back in the book of matches.

Do not touch them yourself!

Ask a spectator to pick up the book and count the matches. He does so. There are still thirteen matches even though you tore out one after he last counted them!

*Even more amazing is the fact that one of them appears to be the dead match that just vanished, and it is still affixed to the book (***13***).*

➤ AFTERTHOUGHTS ◀

If you do not feel confident enough to use the "Shake Vanish" that I have just described, use the "Voodoo Vanish" or "Sitting-Down Vanish" explained earlier in this book. They are basically coin vanishes but are just as suitable for any small object.

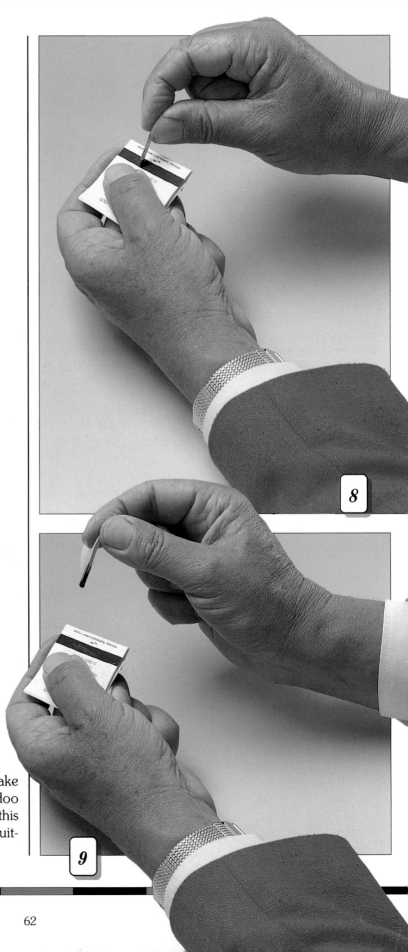

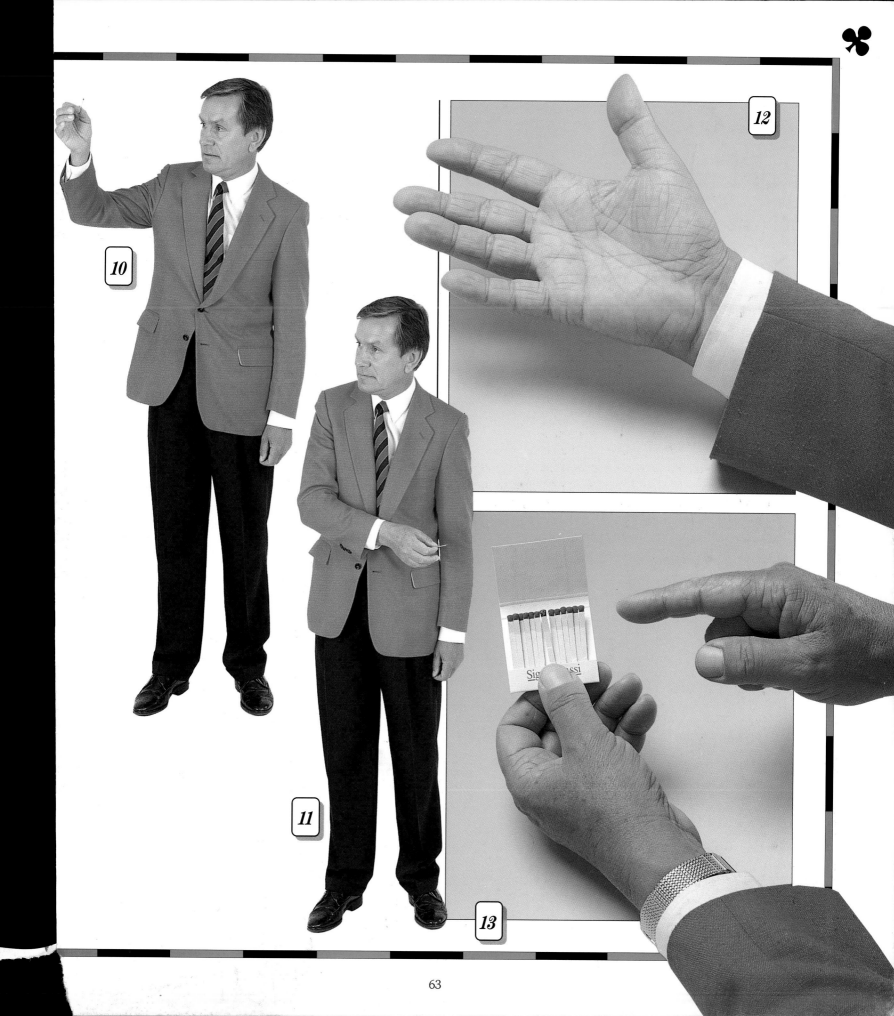

PART FOUR

ROPE MAGIC

THE KNOT THAT IS NOT!

There is an old saying that goes, "Give him enough rope and he will hang himself". Well, with enough rope or string you need not fear hanging yourself – rather you will be able to do this inexplicable trick.

♣ EFFECT ♣

You form a "figure-of-eight" with a length of rope or piece of string and finish it off securely with three or four knots at the top. The spectator is given the figure-of-eight. You explain that the problem is to undo the loop in the centre so that you end up with a plain circle of rope. This feat must be accomplished *without undoing the knots at the top*! However much he plays with and manipulates the rope, he fails to remove the middle loop. You (oh wise one) take back the figure-of-eight and succeed in removing the loop in a fraction of a second.

REQUIREMENTS
A length of rope or string about
2m long

❦ WHAT YOU DO ❧

Take the rope and tie a simple loop in it (**1**). Tie a couple of knots in the ends of the rope to form the figure-of-eight (**2**). Leave the ends long enough so that you can now offer them to the spectator to tie a few more knots himself (**3**). Now explain the "problem" to him. His task is to remove the centre loop without undoing the knots at the top. He will fail dismally. Why? Because it is impossible!

Well our motto is "The *impossible* we do at once – *miracles* take a little longer!" So, as this is only "impossible", we can do it at once. How! We cheat! After his vain attempt to remove the loop, you take back the rope (**4**) and turn your back on him for a second.

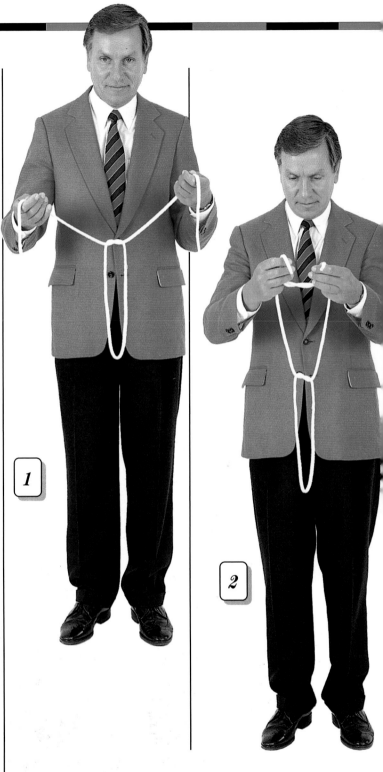

All you have to do is work the centre loop down (**5**) until it joins the knots at the bottom (**6**). One more knot there will never be noticed, believe me (**7**)!

Do not be too quick about it. Make it look as if the feat requires considerable skill. At the end, undo all the knots, reform the figure-of-eight again and leave the rope with him!

3

4

5

6

7

THE SNIP

The cut and restored rope trick has long been a favourite among magicians. Some beautiful routines have been created. Here is a simple but very effective method of performing this classic trick.

◆ EFFECT ◆

A rope that you have clearly cut in half is magically made whole again.

REQUIREMENTS
A length of rope (or string) about
2m long
A pair of sharp scissors

♣ PREPARATION ♣

Put the scissors in your right pocket.

◆ WHAT YOU DO ◆

Display the rope between your hands (**1**). Transfer the right end into your left hand alongside the other end (**2, 3**). You are now apparently going to lift up the centre of the rope and place it alongside these two ends – I did say *apparently*! What actually happens is you lift up the centre, letting it drape over your right index finger and thumb (**4**) and raise it towards your left hand. As soon as it is hidden from the spectators' view by the back of your left hand, grip the right hand rope between your index finger and thumb (**5**) and pull some of that into view instead (**6**). The *true* centre is now hidden by your left hand but it looks as if you have lain it beside the other two ends (**7**).

Take the scissors out of your right jacket pocket and snip through the centre of the visible loop (**8, 9**).

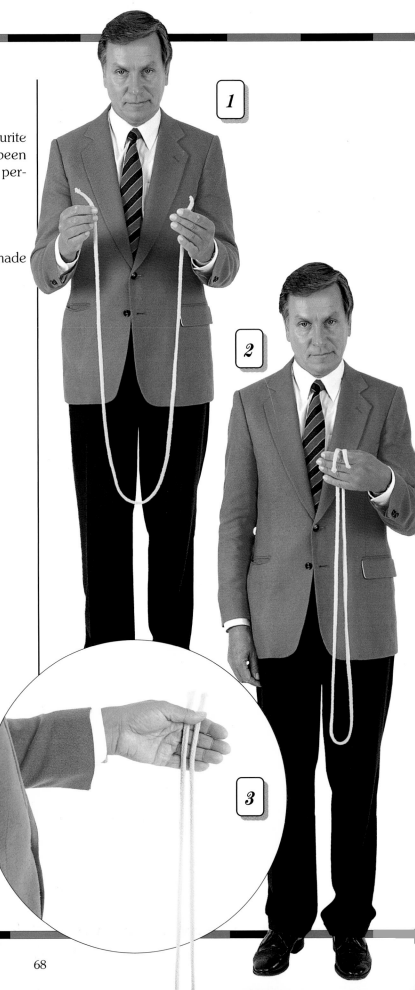

Four ends now show (**10**). Hang on to the two center ends and let the other two drop (**11**). It looks as if you are holding two equal lengths of rope when, in fact, you are holding one long piece linked to a very short piece (**12**). Put the scissors away in your pocket. *This is important* – you will see why later.

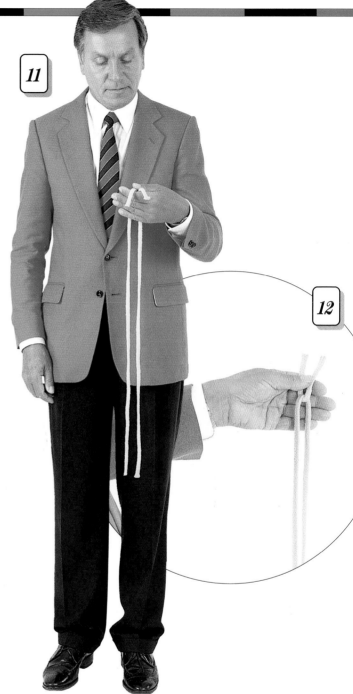

You must now tie the top visible ends together in a double knot. The back of your hand still conceals the hidden loop. What you actually do is tie the little rope on to the center of the long one (**13**). The appearance is now of two equal lengths of rope tied together. Let the complete set up dangle from your left hand (**14**). Remove the scissors from your pocket and trim off most of the protruding ends of the knot (**15, 16, 17**).

Hang on with your left hand and with your right hand, still holding the scissors, start to wind the rope around your left hand (**18**). Keep winding (**19**), until the complete rope is now wound around your left hand (**20**). You will have found that the small piece of rope that was forming the "knot" (**21**) will have slid right off the rope (**22**) and is now concealed in your right fingers and is further hidden by the scissors! This hand immediately goes to your right pocket, where it drops the scissors, and, of course, the knot. That gets rid of the "evidence!" Apparently you have wound the knot into your left hand. Slowly unravel the rope from your left hand (**23**) to show that it has somehow been magically restored (**24**)!

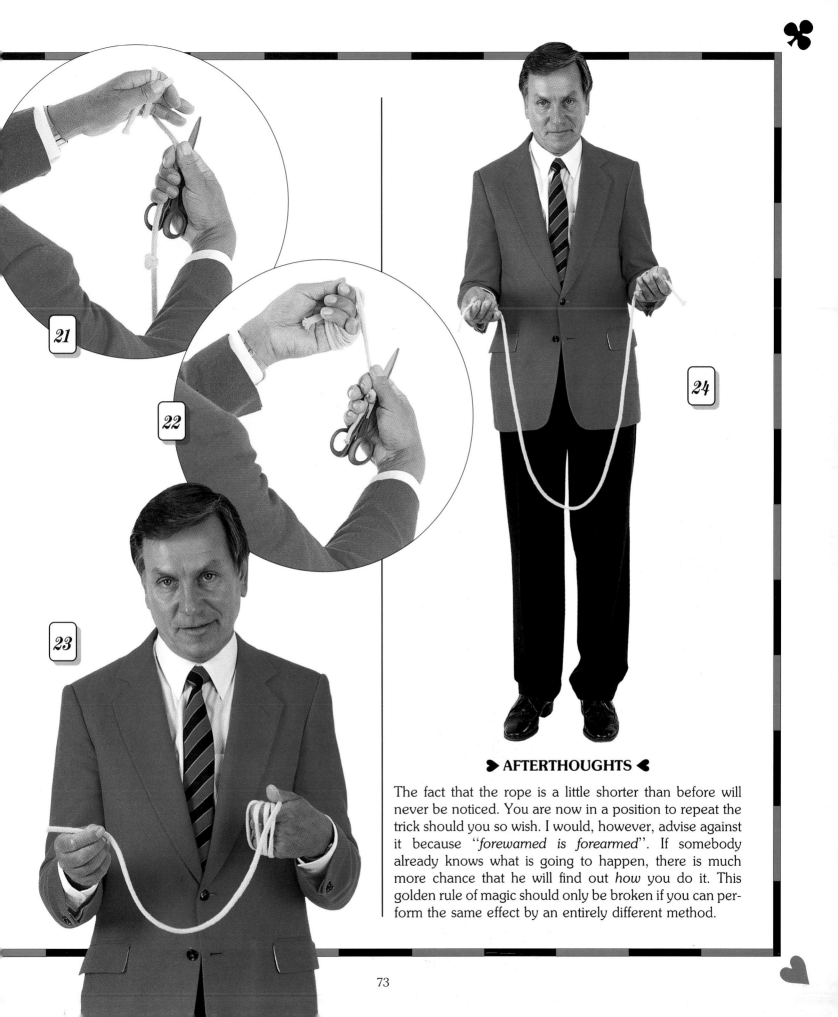

➤ AFTERTHOUGHTS ◄

The fact that the rope is a little shorter than before will never be noticed. You are now in a position to repeat the trick should you so wish. I would, however, advise against it because "*forewarned is forearmed*". If somebody already knows what is going to happen, there is much more chance that he will find out *how* you do it. This golden rule of magic should only be broken if you can perform the same effect by an entirely different method.

HOW LONG IS A PIECE OF ROPE?

This is a real "gem". It never ceases to amaze me that such a simple principle can have such a devastating effect on an audience. They will literally gawp at this one!

♣ EFFECT ♣

Three ropes of dramatically different lengths are shown to, and examined by, the audience. Suddenly, they become all the same length and are clearly seen to be so. In an instant they change back to their original unequal lengths. No trace of the "method" can be found.

REQUIREMENTS
3 pieces of rope (or string)
A spectator – let us call him Clive

B · C · A

◀ PREPARATION ▶

You need to cut the ropes to specific lengths. The first piece (**A**) should be about as long as the distance between your outstretched arms. The second piece (**B**) should be about 25cm long. The third piece (**C**) should be *half* as long as the long piece (**A**) plus *half* the length of the short piece (**B**). Photograph (**1**) should make this clear. Link the long and short ones together so that you get the exact measurement for the third rope. The correct proportions are *vital*!

Please note that we have used ropes of different colours for the reveal shots in this routine. This is simply so that you can see exactly what happens. Obviously, in performance, all the ropes should be of the same colour.

◆ WHAT YOU DO ◆

Hold the three ropes out towards Clive as if offering them to him.

"If you would like to examine these three ropes Clive . . . (Pause) . . . I would be much obliged if you would mind your own business!"

This gets a laugh – but relent anyway and have Clive examine them carefully. Take the ropes back and hold them in your left hand.

"A question that has puzzled people for centuries is . . . 'How long is a piece of rope?'"

Take the longest one away in your right hand (**2**).

"Some people say that a piece of rope is about *this* long . . ."

Take the second one across (**3**).

"Other people say it is *this* long."

Take the smallest one across (**4**).

"Still other people swear that a piece of rope is only *this* long! I think that Confucius had it right. He said that 'how long' was a Chinaman! To a magician, however, all ropes are the same length . . . which is the distance between its opposite ends! Let me show you . . ."

Put the ropes back in your left hand again (**5**, **6**, **7**).

Reach across – *behind* the long one and *in front of* the middle one – to grip the short rope by its lower end (**8, 9**). Lift it up and deposit it in the hollow of your left thumb so that it lies next to its other end (**10**). This secretly links the smallest rope around the longest rope (**11**). Bring up the other two bottom ends and lay them to the *right* (**12, 13, 14, 15**).

"If all the ends are equal – the ropes must be equal too!"

Grasp the first three ends in your right hand and keep hold of the last three ends with your left hand (**16, 17**).

Now pull *slowly* in opposite directions (**18, 19**). The three ropes appear visibly to change to the same length (**20**). The effect is very magical! Drop the ends that you are holding in your right hand and display the ropes in your left hand. Photograph (**21**) shows the spectators' view.

"The three ropes have changed back to their original size again. We have a long one – a medium one – and a very small one!"

Count them back into your right hand (**24, 25, 26**). Drop the ropes on the table so that they may be examined if the spectators so wish. They will wish!

"That's how long a magician's piece of rope is! But then we can do the impossible! Possibly your eyes have been deceiving you because . . ."

Push your right index finger and thumb through the loops as shown (**22, 23**), and pull downwards. The short rope will now come clear as you take the long rope away. Quickly replace the long rope back in your left hand with the other two before Clive has a chance to focus upon it.

➤ AFTERTHOUGHTS ◀

Practise until you can execute the simple moves smoothly. Use a mirror to see how everything looks from the audience's point of view. Do not rush anything. The beauty of this trick lies in the slow, deliberate way that you perform it. And I stress, to make this description clear, we have used three different coloured ropes in some of the photographs. It goes without saying that in actual performance the ropes *must* be all the same colour!

RING OFF

A ring, a piece of string and a handkerchief are all you require to perform this simple but effective trick.

◀ EFFECT ➤

A ring is borrowed from a spectator. You thread and knot it on to a piece of string. You magically remove the ring even though both ends of the string are being held by the spectator!

REQUIREMENTS
A finger ring, which should be borrowed for best effect
A piece of string about 1m long
A linen handkerchief

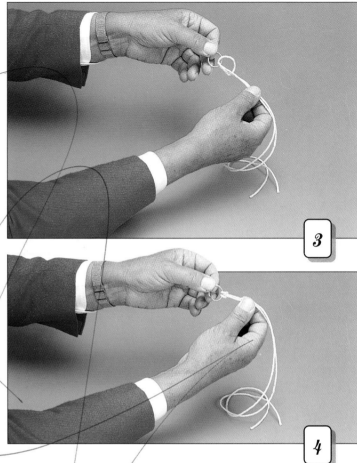

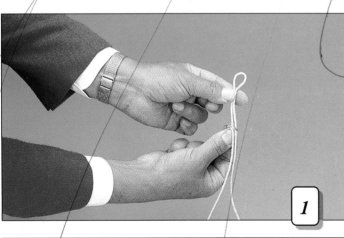

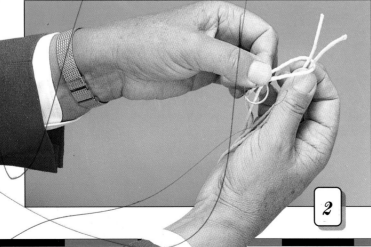

♣ WHAT YOU DO ♣

Having borrowed a substantial looking ring, you thread and tie it onto the string. The "special knot" is our secret because it is not a knot at all! This false knot can be tied in front of the spectator provided that you are very casual about it and do not let her look too closely! Push the *centre* of the string through the ring (**1**) and then feed the loose ends through the loop (**2**), tighten (**3**) and work the knot down to the bottom (**4**). Hold an end of the string in each hand and display the ring, apparently securely tied to its centre. Hand the set-up to the spectator to hold in the same way (**5**).

"While you are holding both ends of the string, it is obviously impossible for me to remove your ring from the string – unless I saw it off!"

Drape the handkerchief over the ring and string (**6**).

"I promise not to do that – instead I will perform a little magic!"

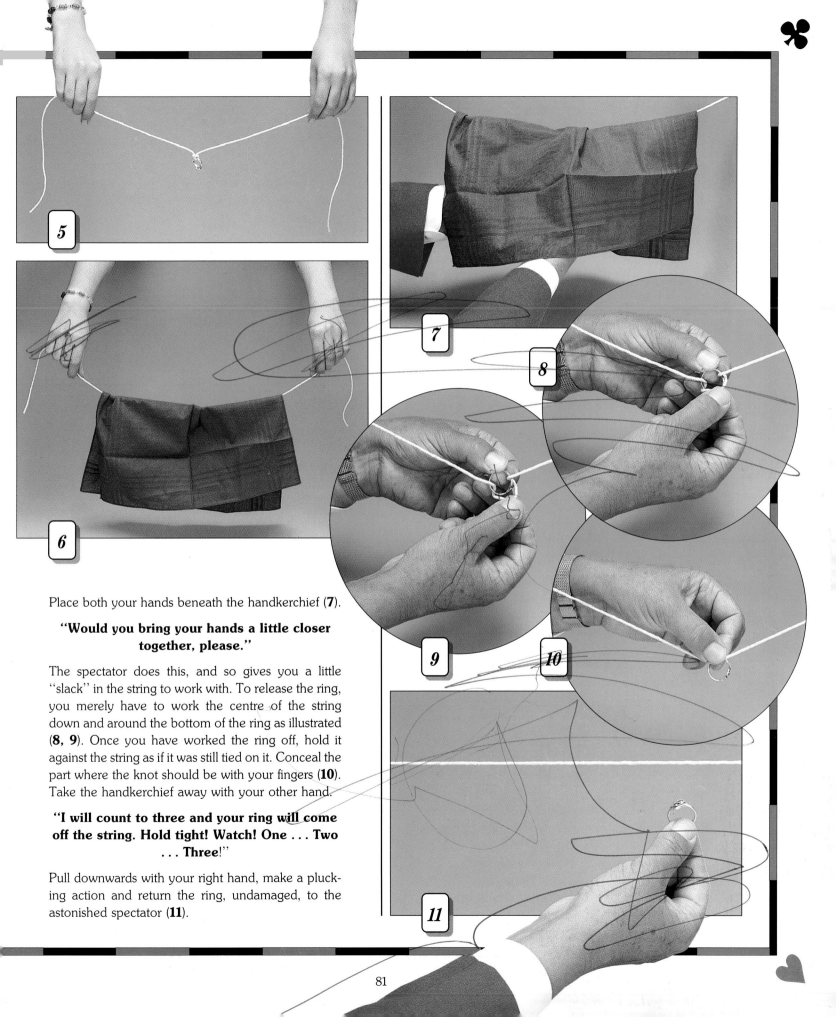

Place both your hands beneath the handkerchief (**7**).

"Would you bring your hands a little closer together, please."

The spectator does this, and so gives you a little "slack" in the string to work with. To release the ring, you merely have to work the centre of the string down and around the bottom of the ring as illustrated (**8, 9**). Once you have worked the ring off, hold it against the string as if it was still tied on it. Conceal the part where the knot should be with your fingers (**10**). Take the handkerchief away with your other hand.

"I will count to three and your ring will come off the string. Hold tight! Watch! One . . . Two . . . Three!"

Pull downwards with your right hand, make a plucking action and return the ring, undamaged, to the astonished spectator (**11**).

MINT OFF

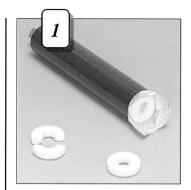

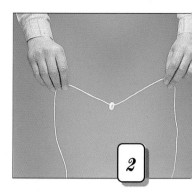

When you are an experienced magician, you often find that your mind works in a peculiar way. You start to think laterally. Only a magician would be crazy enough to think of this next trick!

➤ EFFECT ◄

The effect is exactly the same as in the last "Ring Off" trick, but the method is completely different. This time you use a peppermint (the type with a hole in the middle) and the spectator threads it on himself!

REQUIREMENTS
A packet of peppermints with holes in the middle
A length of string
A linen handkerchief or napkin

◆ PREPARATION ◆

Snap a peppermint in two. Keep trying until you get one with a nice break (**1**). Now moisten the ends and push the two halves together again and allow the peppermint to dry. If the join still shows, try rubbing a little powdered sugar over the cracks. Place another unprepared mint in your right jacket pocket together with a clean handkerchief. Put your "special" mint back in its packet and you are ready to begin.

◄ WHAT YOU DO ➤

Give the string to the spectator. Carefully prise the peppermint out of the packet and let the spectator thread it on the string. As soon as it is on, have him hold the ends of the string as before. This prevents him from examining the mint too closely (**2**)! Remove the handkerchief from your pocket and at the same time palm the unprepared mint and bring that out too, secretly concealed in your curled fingers.

Drape the handkerchief over the string and the visible mint (**3**). Place both your hands beneath the handkerchief (**4**) and snap the threaded peppermint

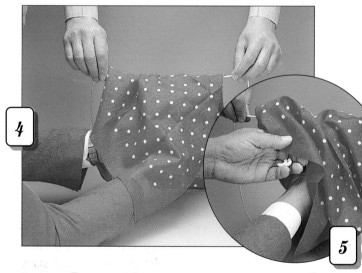

in two. Because of your secret preparation it will break *silently*! Place the pieces in your *left* hand (**5**). Hold the unprepared mint against the string with your *right* hand (**6**). Take the handkerchief away with your left hand and put it away in your left pocket (together with the broken pieces)! Finish by apparently plucking the visible peppermint off the centre of the string (**7**) and immediately handing it to the spectator to examine!

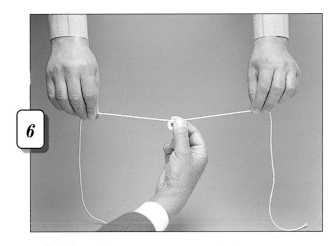

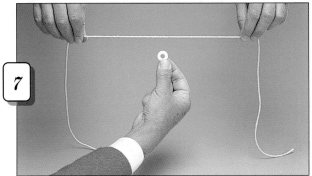

♣ A NICE VARIATION ♣

Once you have learned to snap a mint in two and re-assemble it undetectably, you can perform this super, quite zany, variation of the Mint Off trick. Snap a pep-permint and stick it together again, linking it through an unprepared mint (**8**)! Snap and reassemble two more peppermints. Keep them separate this time and, when they are dry, put them both back in the packet again. Place the linked mints in your *right* jacket pocket together with the handkerchief.

Remove the two mints from the packet and let the spectator thread them on the string and then hold the ends (**9**). Now proceed exactly as before. Break *both* the threaded mints. Take the pieces secretly away with the handkerchief (**10**), which you dump in your left pocket. Now pluck the two mints off the string (**11**) and give them to the spectator (**12**). His face should be a picture because, not only have you removed the two mints, but in the process you have somehow linked them together. Grab the mints back after a while and eat the evidence!

Stunning magic!

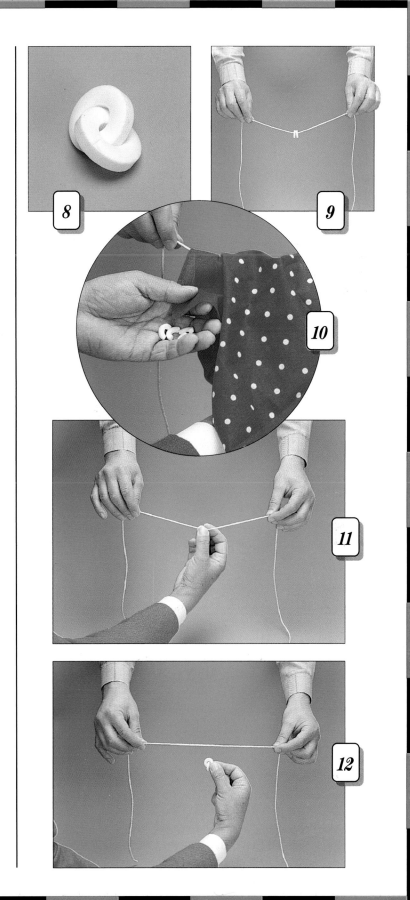

83

THE GIZMO

History has it that in 1626 the Dutch settlers paid the Native Americans little more than a few beads for the island of Manhattan. Now, for the same sort of investment, you can perform a whole host of fascinating tricks!

◆ EFFECT ▶

A piece of cord is apparently able to pass through solid objects without damaging them. For instance, a borrowed ring is threaded on to a length of cord. Even though the spectator still keeps a hold on the ring, the cord penetrates right through it!

REQUIREMENTS
A Gizmo – see the instructions below

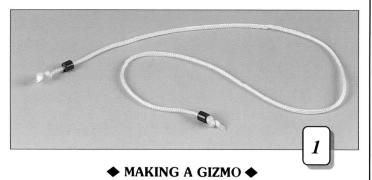

◆ MAKING A GIZMO ◆

You will need to make a "Gizmo". Once made, this simple prop will enable you to do many penetration effects – five of which we will shortly describe.

Buy two beads and a length of nylon cord or smooth string about half a metre long. The beads need be no more than 5mm in circumference. The holes must be large enough and the cord sufficiently thin to enable the beads, once threaded on the cord, to slide along it *freely*. Thread the two beads on the cord and tie a large knot at each end so that the beads cannot fall off. Your "life-long" prop is complete. You have made a Gizmo (**1**).

▶ PREPARATION ◀

You will need to practise a technique known as the stroke. The object is secretly to transfer one bead to the opposite end of the cord so that you end up with *both* beads at the same end. That is why it is important that the holes in the beads are large enough to allow them to slide freely and also why the cord must be smooth. The bead is transferred in the action of *stroking* the cord.

Start with one bead at each end. Hold one bead between your right thumb and index finger (**2**). With your left thumb and index finger start at the top (as close to the right thumb and index finger as possible) and stroke downwards (**3**) until you reach the bottom bead (**4**). This stroking action (almost like someone toying with their worry beads) should be repeated three or four times so that the spectator gets acclimatized to the action.

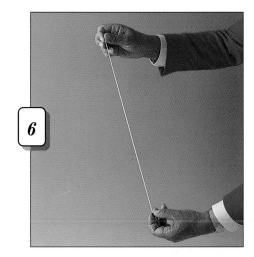

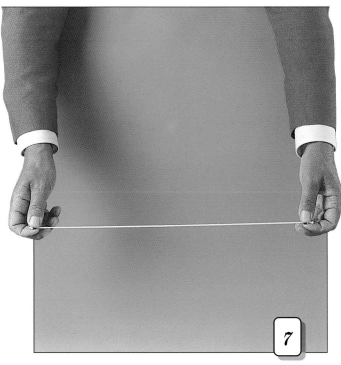

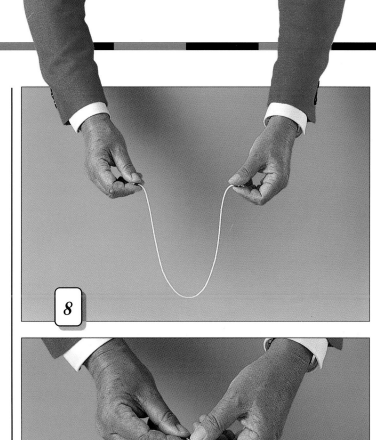

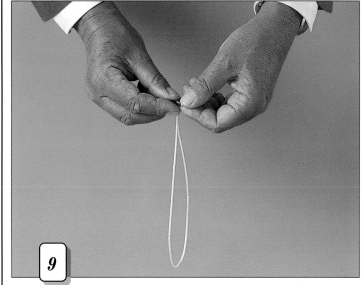

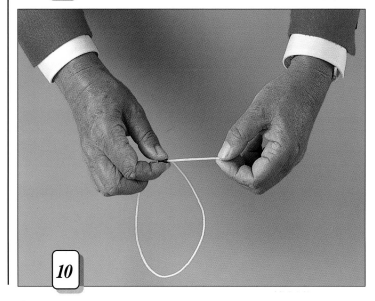

When you are ready secretly to transfer the bead across, stroke as before, only this time, when you reach the top bead, grip it between your left finger and thumb (**5**). While your right hand hangs on to the knot, your left hand can transfer the bead from the top to the bottom of the cord (**6**). Another method of transfer can be used when the Gizmo is held horizontally (**7**). Start to bring your hands together (**8**) and when they touch, allow the right finger and thumb to grip the left hand bead too (**9**). The left finger and thumb grip the left *knot* and pull it away (**10**), leaving the two beads held in your right hand (**11**).

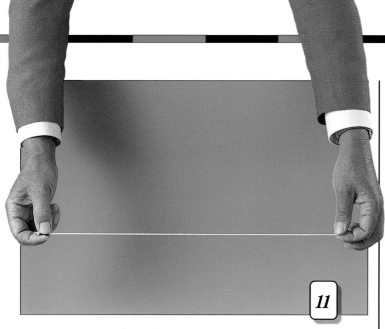

11

13

♣ WHAT YOU DO ♣

◆ TRICK 1 ◆

While in position (**11**), get someone to place her arm on top of the cord (**12**). Reverse the last action, bringing your hands together *above* her arm, and take back the bead with your left finger and thumb again (**13**). Let the knot drop and at the same time pull your hands *sharply* in opposite directions (**14**). The cord will "whip" around the other side of her arm quicker than the eye can possibly follow and you will end up in position (**15**) with a bead at each end of the cord which is now above her arm!

Apparently it has penetrated right through!

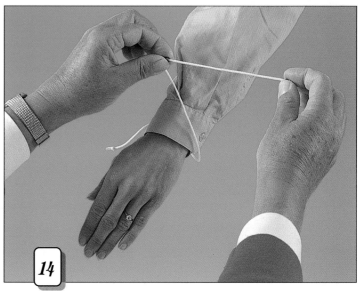

14

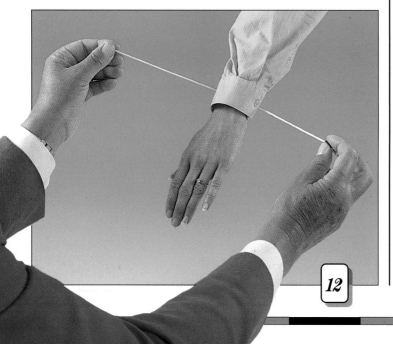

12

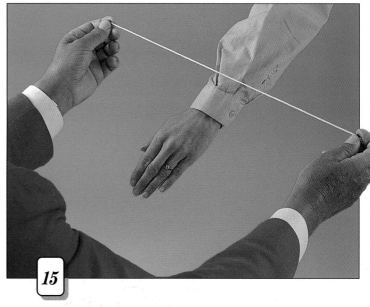

15

86

◄ TRICK 2 ►

Practise on your own leg. Sit on a chair. Do the stroke bead transfer. Place the cord beneath your leg (**16**). Bring the ends of the Gizmo up and over your leg. Transfer one bead back to your left hand again and then *pull*. If you have not chopped your leg off, the cord will appear to have penetrated through your leg (**17**).

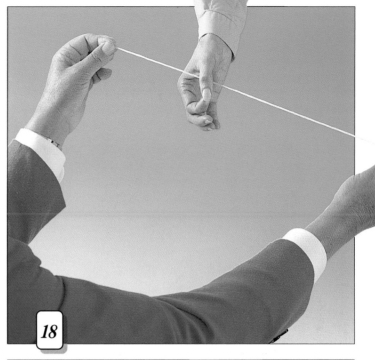

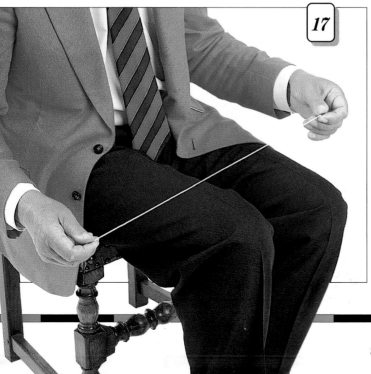

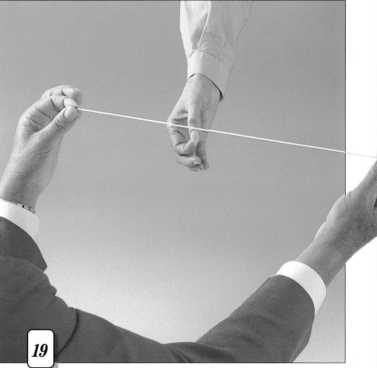

► TRICK 3 ◄

Make the bead transfer. Get someone to hold her index finger and thumb very firmly together in an "O" shape around the cord (**18**). Escape from her clutches in the usual way (**19**)!

♣ TRICK 4 ♣

Hold the Gizmo behind your neck (**20**) making the bead transfer as you do this. Bring the ends of the Gizmo to the front. Transfer the bead again and *pull forward*. Watch out – your head has just fallen off! No, all is fine (**21**)!

◀ TRICK 5 ▶

The handling here is slightly different but the technique is the same. Hold both ends of the Gizmo between the forefinger and thumb of your right hand, borrow a ring from a lady and momentarily lay it over the beads as shown (**22**). With your left hand reach into the ring and pinch the knot of the bead nearest your fingertips. Now pull away to your left (**23**), keeping hold of the beads with your right hand (**24**), and letting the ring hang on the center of the cord (**25**). Ask a spectator to grip the edge of her ring very firmly (**26**). Bring your hands together (**27**) and escape from the ring (**28**)!

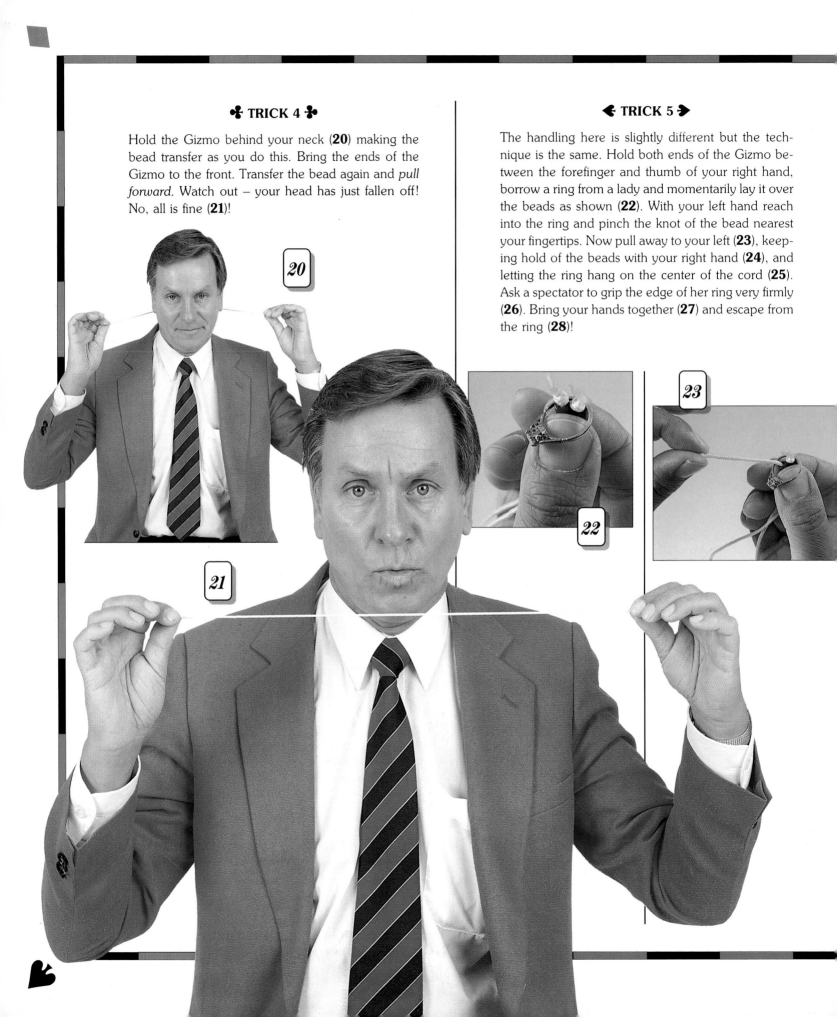

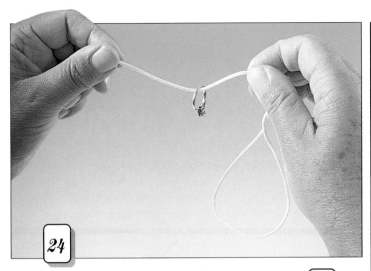

24

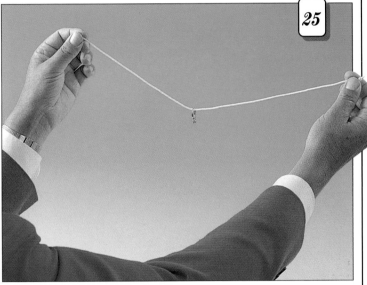

25

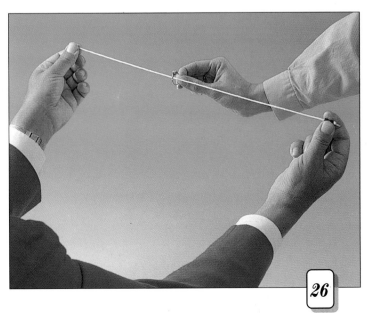

26

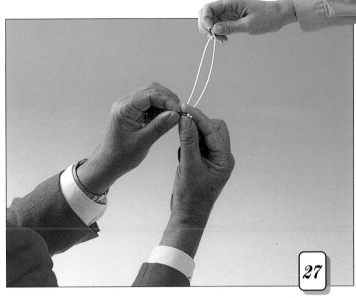

27

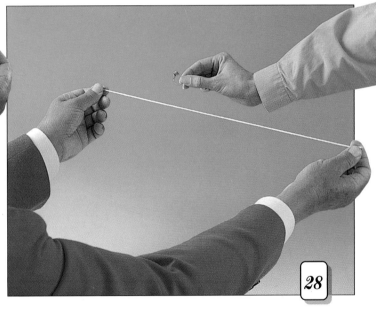

28

❯ AFTERTHOUGHTS ❮

I am sure that you will find many more ways to use your Gizmo. It will penetrate through anything that it can be wrapped around – in other words anything that has a circumference shorter than the length of your Gizmo.

I use my Gizmo for other tricks that just need a piece of cord or string e.g. "Ring Off", "Mint Off" etc. By doing this, the spectators get used to seeing the Gizmo around. Build a little routine of two or three tricks and just use the bead transfer feature in the final one. *Do not use the Gizmo more than once.* Remember our Golden Rule? Forewarned is Forearmed!

PART FIVE

MIND MAGIC

SOME CHANCE!

People love a little gamble and any trick where your audience appears to have a chance of winning money will always be well received. However, when a magician says "Some Chance!", he usually means "No Chance!" This trick is no exception!

♣ EFFECT ♣

You show five envelopes and state that one, and only one, of them contains a banknote. You allow four spectators freely to choose an envelope. They can swap as often as they like. You tell them that if they get the envelope that contains the money, *they can keep it*! Needless to say, they always leave you with the envelope containing the note! We hope!

REQUIREMENTS
Five letter-size envelopes
Five transparent pay envelopes
A banknote – the more valuable,
the better!

➤ PREPARATION ➤

Insert a transparent envelope inside each of the envelopes so that the end of it which opens is at the top as you lift the flap of the letter envelope. Fold the banknote in half, and then in half again the same way. Finally fold the note in half once the other way. This will result in a folded note about 3cm square which opens at one side. Pick up the five envelopes in your left hand and hold them so that the flaps are away from you, to your right. Clip the banknote over the left hand edge of the second envelope from the bottom (**1**) about a third of the way up. Place the envelopes on the table in a pile with the edge of the note nearest to you so that it is unseen by the spectators.

◆ WHAT YOU DO ◆

"I have five envelopes here and one of them contains a banknote."

Pick up the stack of envelopes and count them from your left hand into your right, keeping the envelopes upright facing the audience. As you count off the third envelope, your left thumb will automatically fall on the note (**2**). As you count off the fourth envelope, your left thumb retains the note and it comes to rest on the address side of the fifth envelope. The fifth envelope is now counted into the right hand too, and your left fingers retain the note hidden from view.

Immediately replace the fan of five envelopes back into your left hand, on top of and thus concealing the note (**3**), which now lies between your fingers and the bottom envelope. You can now show the fan of envelopes on both sides. Do not make a big "thing" of it. Practise these simple moves until they become smooth. Remember that, to your audience, you have merely counted five envelopes from hand to hand and you must make this action appear perfectly natural.

"I want four people each to choose an envelope, leaving me with one. You can choose any envelope that you wish and if you get the one that contains the money – you can keep it! Promise!"

Advance to the first spectator and have him remove one envelope from the fan. Slightly relax your grip on the envelopes and he will be able to draw one out cleanly without disturbing the spread. You will find it an easy matter to conceal the note under the envelopes even if he chooses the one nearest your palm, because, as he removes it, it will slide past the note which will automatically remain against the back of the next envelope. As soon as he has made his choice, say . . .

"Would you like to change your mind?"

He will usually say, "No", but if he accepts your invitation, take his envelope from him, replace it on top of the fan, and then offer the five envelopes for him to make a second selection. Have the other three envelopes chosen in the same way – each time giving the spectators the opportunity to change their minds – emphasising always the "fairness" of it all!

You are now left with one envelope in your left hand, under which is concealed the folded note. Change the grip of your left hand so that you hold the envelope clipped between your first and second fingers, with the note between the envelope and your second finger (**4**). The reveal shot (**5**) shows how you should hold the note concealed from view.

"Please open your envelopes and see who has won the money!"

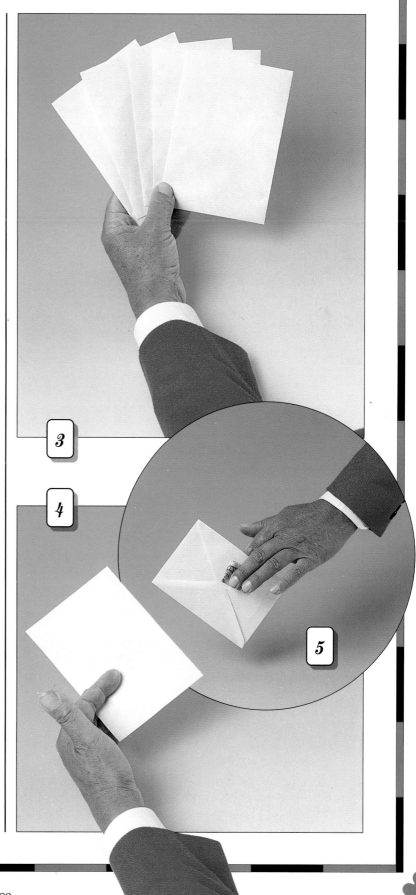

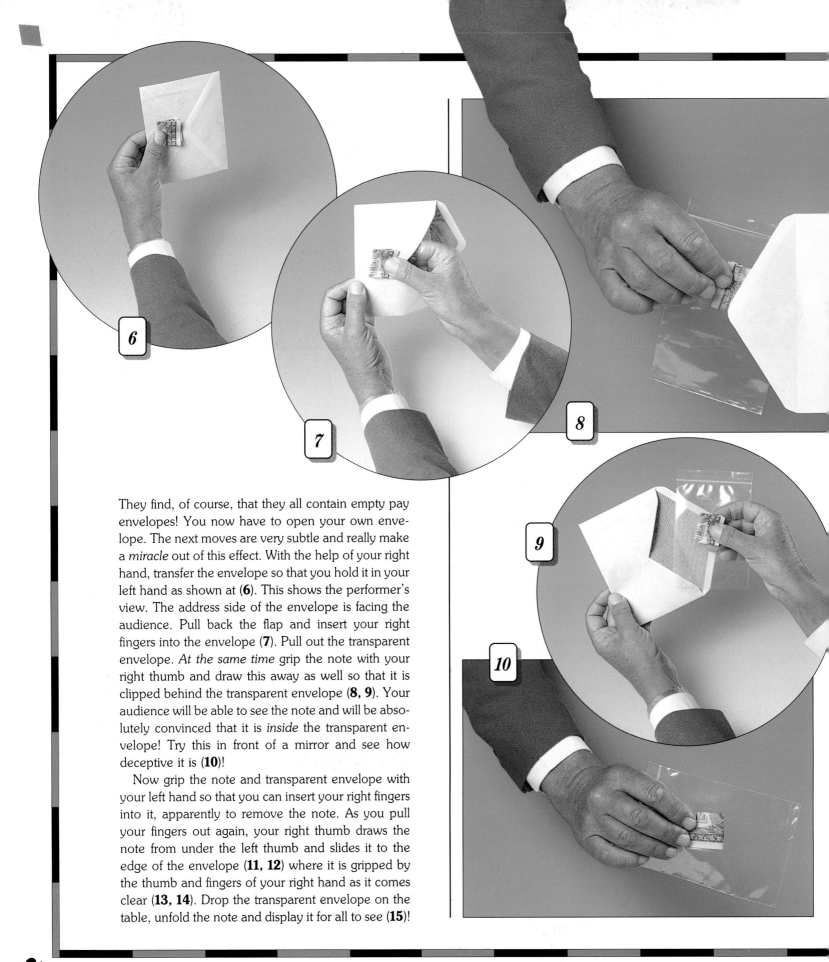

They find, of course, that they all contain empty pay envelopes! You now have to open your own envelope. The next moves are very subtle and really make a *miracle* out of this effect. With the help of your right hand, transfer the envelope so that you hold it in your left hand as shown at (**6**). This shows the performer's view. The address side of the envelope is facing the audience. Pull back the flap and insert your right fingers into the envelope (**7**). Pull out the transparent envelope. *At the same time* grip the note with your right thumb and draw this away as well so that it is clipped behind the transparent envelope (**8, 9**). Your audience will be able to see the note and will be absolutely convinced that it is *inside* the transparent envelope! Try this in front of a mirror and see how deceptive it is (**10**)!

Now grip the note and transparent envelope with your left hand so that you can insert your right fingers into it, apparently to remove the note. As you pull your fingers out again, your right thumb draws the note from under the left thumb and slides it to the edge of the envelope (**11, 12**) where it is gripped by the thumb and fingers of your right hand as it comes clear (**13, 14**). Drop the transparent envelope on the table, unfold the note and display it for all to see (**15**)!

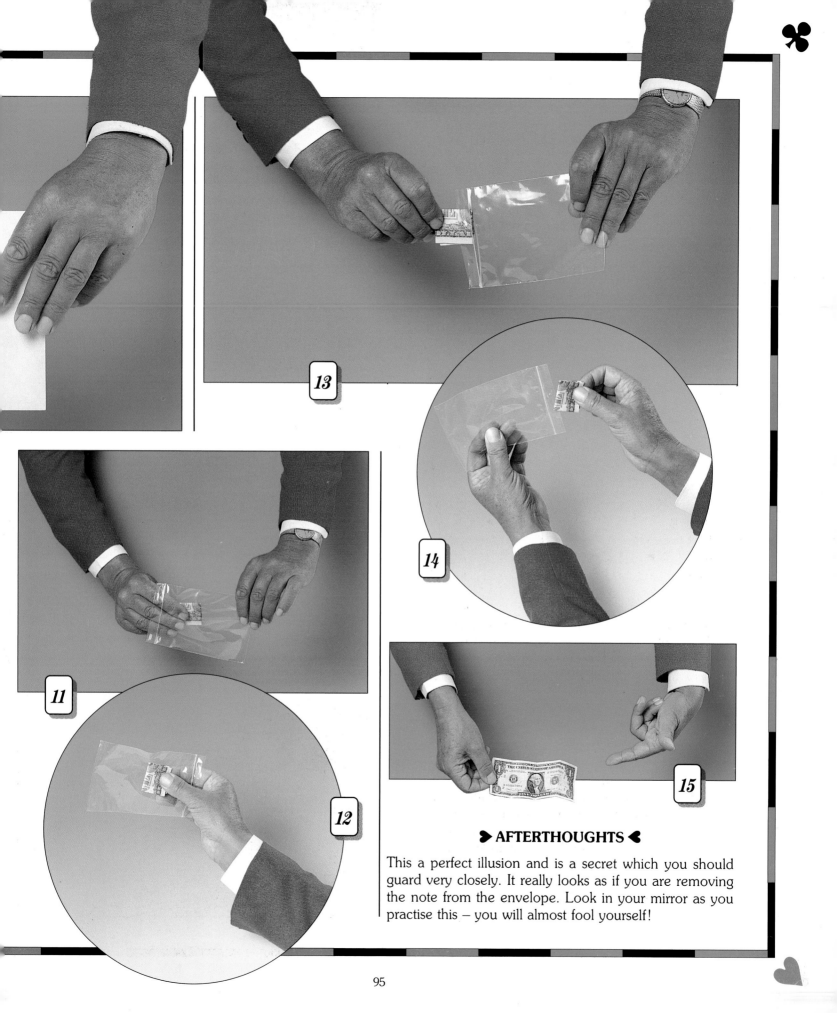

13

14

11

12

15

❥ AFTERTHOUGHTS ❧

This a perfect illusion and is a secret which you should guard very closely. It really looks as if you are removing the note from the envelope. Look in your mirror as you practise this – you will almost fool yourself!

SENSITIVE FINGERS

People want to believe that there is something in astrology. People want to believe in the supernatural. People want to believe that it is possible for someone to read their minds. Far be it from us to disappoint our audience!

◆ EFFECT ◆

From a full box of coloured crayons, a spectator secretly removes one and hands it to you to hold behind your back. After a moment's concentration, and without looking at it, you correctly tell her the colour of the crayon that you are holding!

REQUIREMENTS
A box of wax crayons. They normally come in sets of nine different colours

---

◆ WHAT YOU DO ◆

Take the crayons out of the box and show that each one is a different colour (**1**).

"I have been able to tune my senses to an amazing degree. I have taught myself to read minds and 'see' with my finger tips. Please let me show you."

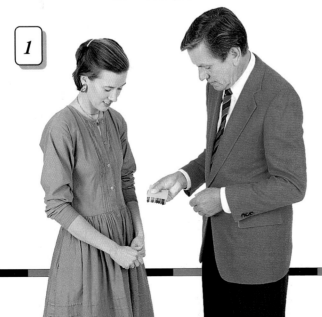

Give the spectator the box of crayons (**2**) and turn your back towards her.

"While my back is turned to you, I want you to choose one of the crayons – any one you like – and place it in my hand. Now place the rest of the crayons back in the box and hide them from my sight. Tell me when you have done that."

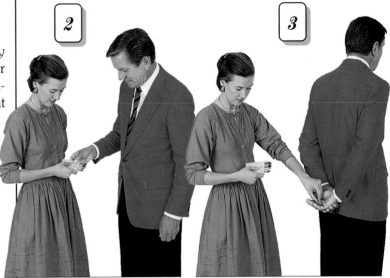

She chooses one, places it in your hand, which is behind your back (**3**), and hides the others as requested. As soon as she tells you that all is ready, you turn around to face her (**4**). As you do this, scrape some of the wax off the top of the crayon with the nail of your right index finger (**5**). Don't go mad – just a minute scrap is all you need!

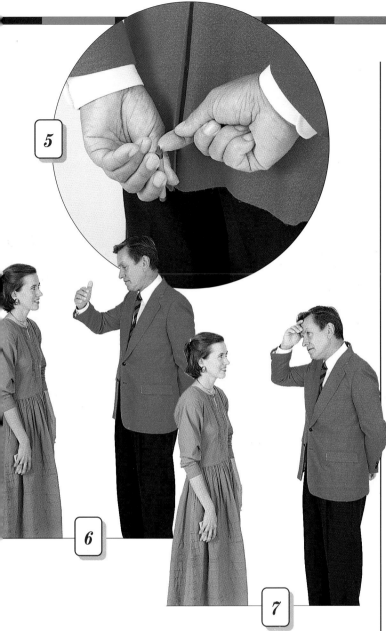

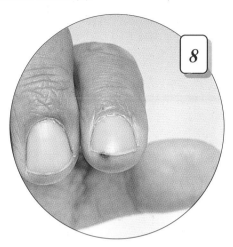

It only remains for you to reveal this knowledge as dramatically as possible. Act it up a bit. Pretend that your fingers are not "seeing" very well today. Ask her to help you out by concentrating very hard on her colour. Tell her that her mind is a blank. Tell her to think harder! Make it look very difficult! Then call out the correct colour (**9**)!

♣ AFTERTHOUGHTS ♣

Pseudo mindreading tricks are best performed on their own and not mixed with other types of tricks. Why? Well, if you have previously presented a dazzling display of sleight-of-hand and then embark upon a mindreading trick, your audience will, quite rightly, assume that this is achieved by sleight-of-hand too. This, of course, defeats our object. There are a handful of mental tricks in this book. Use two or three of them and link them into a mental routine. Never say that you do read minds and never say you do not! Let your audience be the judge.

"I want you to think of the colour that you have chosen. Don't say it out loud – just think of it."

Still holding the crayon in your left hand behind your back, bring your *right* hand forward and slowly up (**6**), and hold it to your forehead as if to help you in your concentration (**7**). This does two things. It shows that your hand is empty but, much more importantly, it enables you secretly to look at your finger nail as your hand passes in front of your eyes en route to your forehead! There, seen only by you, is a minute scrap of coloured crayon (**8**). This tells you the colour of the crayon that you are holding behind your back! Very crafty!

THE HAUNTED KEY

I love weird tricks. This one is extremely weird and I have had a lot of fun with it over the years! Eat your heart out, Uri Geller!

◆ EFFECT ◆

A large, heavy key is laid across your palm. Merely by "concentration" you cause it to come alive and turn itself right over! The key is immediately handed out for examination. No trace of the method can be found. It must be haunted!

REQUIREMENTS
The largest, heaviest mortise key that you can find (**1**). Strangely enough, the larger and heavier the key, the easier and yet more spectacular the trick is.

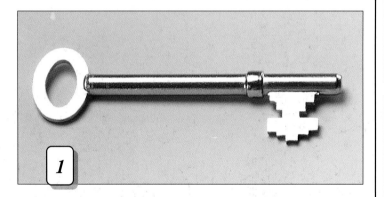

◀ WHAT YOU DO ▶

This is a "knack" really. It will take a little practice but just like riding a bicycle, it will suddenly come to you. Lay the key across your right palm. The exact position is very important (**2**). Notice that the flat part that is normally inserted into the lock is pointing back towards your wrist. The other end of the key that has the ring on it must be "free" and not resting on your hand at all. Look down on your hand.

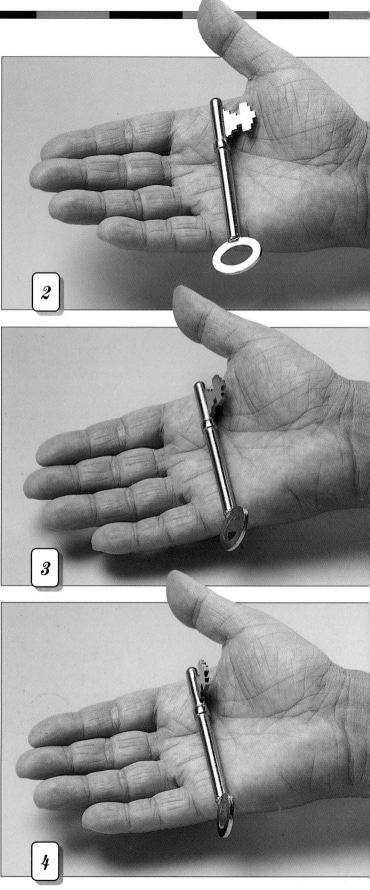

Very, very slightly dip your fingers towards the floor and, at the same time, *will* the key to turn over! I know that sounds daft but it really helps! Slowly and mysteriously the key turns itself over (**3, 4, 5, 6**)! At first you will probably find that the key will roll over very quickly and probably end up on the floor! However, with a little practice, and by varying the degree that you tip your fingers, you will be able to control the movement of the key completely so that it turns over very slowly, spookily and inexplicably! Try it! You'll have fun!

5

6

➤ AFTERTHOUGHTS ◄

Many hotels or bars that are decorated with horse brasses also hang decorative brass keys on their walls. If you can, borrow one of these and cause a sensation with this trick. Uri Geller did!

Part Six

Magic Miscellany

SHORT AND SWEET!

You will not always be able to perform this trick. However, when the conditions are right, it is an absolute stunner and well worth remembering!

♣ EFFECT ♣

Somebody hands you a wrapped sugar cube packet from the bowl on the table. You place the packet on the back of your hand and tap it smartly with the other hand. The sugar cubes penetrate through your palm and plop into the coffee cup – leaving the crumpled wrapper on top of your hand!

REQUIREMENTS
Just two packets of wrapped
sugar cubes

◆ PREPARATION ◆

When you find yourself in a restaurant that leaves wrapped sugar cubes on the table, secretly pocket one. Then excuse yourself to the lavatory. Once in private there, carefully unwrap the sugar cubes (**1**). Put them in your pocket and then carefully reassemble the wrapper again. Moisten the adhesive flap and you will find that very likely it will stick down again, and the packet will resume its former shape even though it is now empty. Keep this empty parcel secretly cupped in your fingers as you return to the table. Be careful not to crush it.

➤ WHAT YOU DO ◄

Palm the sugar cubes in your left hand. The empty packet is carefully palmed in your right fingers. As soon as coffee has been served and before anyone can reach for the sugar you say, apparently on the spur of the moment (**2**),

"I've just had an idea for a trick – let's see if it works – does anyone take sugar?" Jane says that she does. **"O.K. Jane. Hand me a packet of sugar, please."**

She hands you a packet of sugar. Take it with your right hand and place it about 10cm from the edge of the table and in line with your lap (**3**). With your right fingers draw the sugar packet towards yourself with a sweeping action (**4**). Let this packet secretly fall into your lap (**5, 6**) and simultaneously bring the *empty* packet into view, placing it on the back of your closed left fist (**7**). Practise this "switch" until you have got it off pat. It should look as if you have just picked up the packet that she has chosen and placed it on the back of your left fist.

Position your left hand above the coffee cup (**8**). Now synchronise these two actions. Tap the wrapper smartly with your right fingers and *at the same time* spring open your left fingers. The two sugar lumps "splash down" into the coffee and the crumpled wrapper is left for examination (**9**). The illusion of the sugar lumps penetrating your hand is perfect. Pocket the lapped sugar packet at your leisure. Short and sweet!

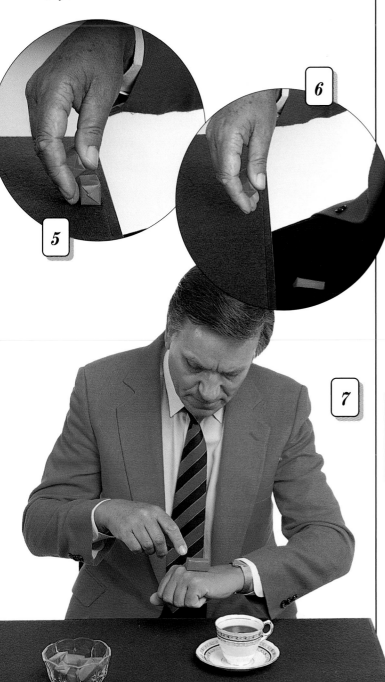

❮ AFTERTHOUGHTS ❯

If nobody in your party takes sugar, perform the trick on your own coffee cup. If *you* do not take sugar either, don't stir it! You will be amazed how effective this little trick is. Just make sure that you do your preparation properly. If you cannot pocket a sugar packet without being seen, do not do the trick. Remember to practise the "switch" until you can do it in your sleep.

OVER THE TOP

With just a few bottle tops you give a demonstration of incredible sleight-of-hand, and it is easier than you think!

♣ EFFECT ♣

Four bottle tops are laid out on the table. One is covered for a split second by your left hand. It instantly disappears, only to be found under your right hand. You cover another. That, too, disappears and reappears instantly beneath your right hand. The last two bottle tops go the way of the first two – until all four bottle tops invisibly travel across.

REQUIREMENTS
Five identical bottle tops – the type that have scalloped edges. The audience only ever sees four!

❧ PREPARATION ☙

You will have to learn to palm a bottle top. The scalloped edges make this a very simple task. Lay a bottle top on the table with its scalloped edges facing upwards. Place your right hand over it so that the bottle top is positioned in the direct centre of your palm (**1**). Press down. Squeeze the sides of your hand inwards. See how little you have to squeeze before the flesh of your palm is able to get a grip on the bottle top. Still keeping your hand flat lift your hand off the table. (**2**). The bottle top stays palmed (**3**). The scalloped edges make this a very easy palm to execute. Practise until you can "palm" with either hand. When you can do that, you are ready to learn this classic routine.

◀ WHAT YOU DO ▶

Sit at a table with your legs tucked well under it. Lay four bottle tops out as shown (**4**). You start with the secret extra top palmed in your *right* hand.

"This is a trick called 'Over The Top'. What's it called?"

Your audience replies . . . "Over The Top".

"That's right. O.T.T. for short! O.T.T. goes like this . . ."

Cover "A" with your left hand and "B" with your right hand (**5**). Wiggle the fingers of both hands up and down a few times. Release the palmed top from your right palm to join "B" which it is covering, and at the same time palm "A" in your left hand. Move both hands away to show that "A" has apparently jumped across to join "B" (**6**). Move one of the tops at "B" back to position "A" again (**7**).

". . . or, sometimes, like this . . ."

Cover "A" and "B" with your hands again (**8**).

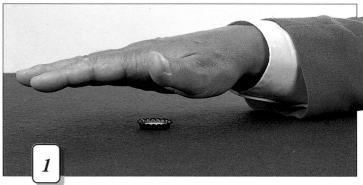

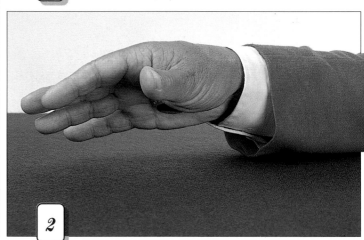

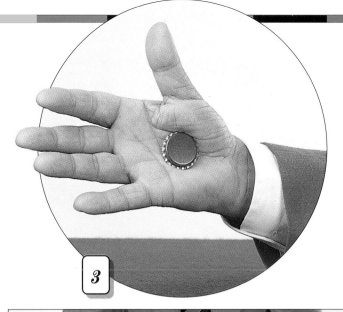

3

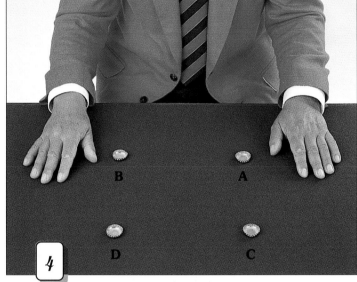

4

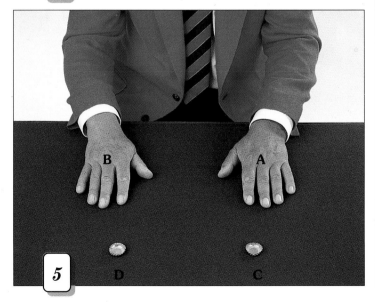

5

6

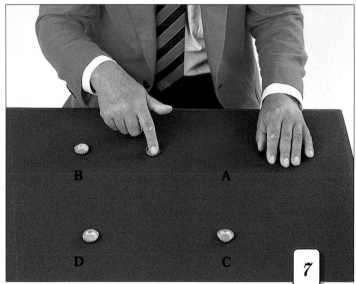

7

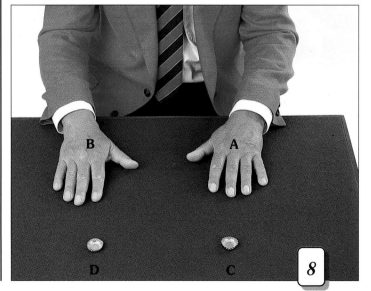

8

Drop the palmed top to join "A" and at the same time palm "B". Wiggle your fingers a little, then move your hands to the sides again. Apparently "B" has jumped over to join "A" (**9**). Move one of the tops at "A" back to position "B" (**10**), once more forming the square.

". . . although it is usually like this . . ."

Cover "A" and "B" again (**11**). Palm "A" and drop at "B". "A" seems to have jumped to "B" again (**12**)

"Sometimes, however, O.T.T. is like this . . ."

Cover position "B" with your *left* hand and reach across to cover position "C" with your *right* hand (**13**). Palm at "C" and drop at "B". Move your hands away (**14**).

"Once in a blue moon, it looks like this . . ."

Cover "D" with your *left* hand and "B" with your *right* (**15**). Palm at "D", drop at "B". Lift your left hand off the table and bring it back to rest on the *edge* of the table above your lap (**16**). Lift up your right hand and turn it, slowly, face upwards. At the same time let the top that is palmed in your left hand drop secretly on to your lap! Then, slowly, turn your left hand face up too! (**17**) You are, as we say, "clean"!

"That's 'Over The Top'!"

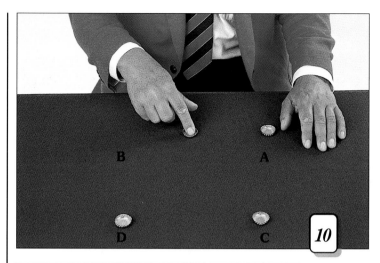

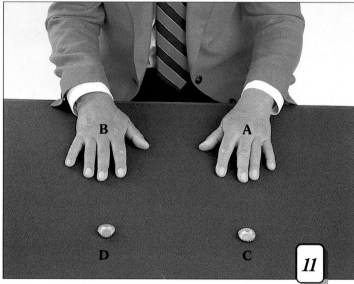

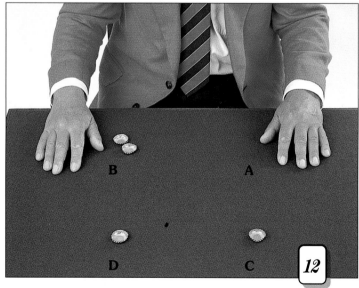

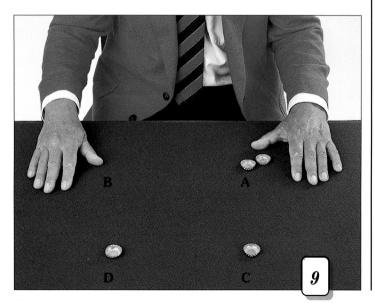

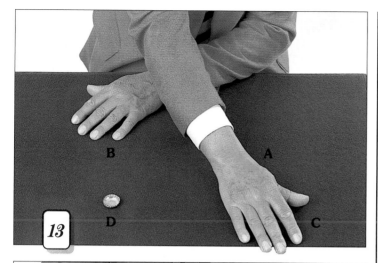

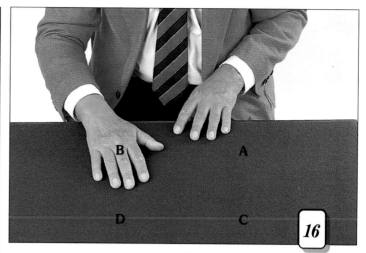

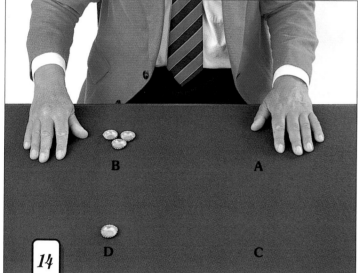

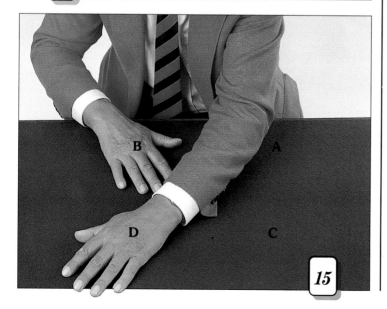

◆ AFTERTHOUGHTS ◆

Once you have taught yourself this routine, and you can perform it smoothly and palm with equal dexterity with either hand, I suggest that you throw the bottle tops away! Try using sugar cubes instead. The "palm" is slightly more difficult but once you have the hang of it, you should be able to palm sugar cubes. Bottle tops are great to practise with, but, unfortunately, the scalloped edges that make them so easy to palm can also give the game away. Nobody imagines that you could possibly palm a flat-sided cube!

PENCIL PUSHER

This trick takes only three seconds to perform, yet is most effective given the right conditions.

♣ EFFECT ♣

A pencil vanishes from your bare hands!

REQUIREMENTS
A pencil, which may be borrowed

◆ WHAT YOU DO ◆

This trick is best performed to just one person. It is 99 per cent *presentation*. Although it is a small trick, you must make a big show of it! Have a pencil ready – borrowed if possible. Stand with the spectator on your *left* (**1**). Hold your left hand palm upwards in front of you. Hold the pencil in the "writing" position in your right hand (**2**). The following moves must be performed in a smooth, rhythmic sequence to the count of "three".

"Watch closely! I will make this pencil pass right through my palm!"

Bending your right arm at the elbow, swing your hand up in an arc until the pencil is level with the top of your right ear (**3**). Bring your hand down again, reversing the arc and press the point of the pencil into the palm of your left hand (**4**). You count "One". Do it again, lift the hand and pencil up to ear level then bring it down again, pressing the pencil into your palm, and counting "Two". Do it again, but this time slide the pencil *behind your ear*. Leave it there and swing the hand down again as if it was still holding the pencil (**6**). Press your fingers into your palms (**7**), and count "Three"! Display both hands empty (**8**). The pencil has disappeared! Try this out. You will be amazed how deceptive it is.

4

7

5

8

6

➤ AFTERTHOUGHTS ◄

This trick works because the spectator's attention is misdirected towards your left palm. The wide arc described by your right hand is too wide for her angle of vision. The pencil is, therefore, out of sight for a fraction of a second.

You can reverse the procedure and make the pencil re-appear. Just retrieve the pencil from behind your ear *after* the count of two. Any long object can be vanished in this way. I have seen it done with a cigarette – unlit of course!

SUPERMAN!

Alex Natus, a businessman from South Africa, only knows two tricks. He showed me this one in 1950! He claimed that he was taught the trick by his father who in turn learned it from his father before him. In his hands it is a "miracle". If you practise, it will be a "miracle" in your hands too!

♣ EFFECT ♣

Three silver balls are manufactured on the spot from silver paper . . . then one ball is pushed into the corner of your eye! Another is pushed into your ear! The third is "massaged" into the back of your neck! The three balls are now magically reproduced one at a time from your mouth. They are all placed in your left hand and then completely disappear!

REQUIREMENTS
A sheet of tin foil paper from a cigarette paper or chocolate bar, which should be borrowed whenever possible.

◀ WHAT YOU DO ▶

All the moves of this routine must be performed *slowly* and gracefully – thus enhancing the truly magical qualities of this trick. Openly and unmistakably tear the foil into three equal-size pieces (**1**, **2**). Roll them into three tight little balls (**3**) and display them on your left palm (**4**).

"I have three little silver balls, which is unusual, even in Sussex . . ." (Change this according to where you live.)

Now close both hands into fists, keeping them about 50cm apart (**5**).

"I am going to try to make the three balls travel from my left hand over here into my right hand! Would you like them to go visibly or invisibly?"

7

8

9

10

If the spectator says, "Visibly", open both hands palm upwards and simply tip the three balls from your left on to your right palm!

"That's 'visibly'! *Invisibly* looks like this . . ."

Tip the balls back on to your left palm. Close both hands into fists again. Make a "throwing" action with your left hand and a "catching" action with your right *but at all times keep your fists tightly closed*. "They are now over here" you say, looking at your right fist but not opening it.

"That was easy, but to make them go back again – that takes a lot more practice!"

Repeat the "throwing" and "catching" actions as before and open both hands (**6, 7**) to show that the three balls have "returned" to the left hand! This preliminary bit of nonsense may sound like a waste of time to you. I assure you that it is not! It impresses on your audience that you are only using *three* balls and that you do not have any more concealed anywhere. Now for the trick proper.

The three balls are displayed on your left palm. Reach over with your right hand with the action of picking up a ball between your fingers (**8**). Actually you secretly pick up *two* balls, one on top of the other. Your left fingers close back into a fist at the same time as your right hand is removed. Hold the right hand up in front of you for a moment. The spectator should only see the top ball (**9**). Place it between your lips (**10**).

11

12

Now . . . we are holding *two* balls remember . . . so this is what *actually* happens: one ball is dropped secretly into your mouth and the second one is left between your lips, openly displayed. Let the ball in your mouth drop beneath your tongue. Do not worry about it. Try to forget that it is there. With a little practice you will be able to leave it there and yet talk unimpaired, drink quite freely, etc. Needless to say, it is imperative that your audience remains unaware of its presence. Now back to the visible ball. With your right index finger roll the ball backwards and forwards along your lips a couple of times and then remove it openly between your index finger and thumb (**11**) and place it, for display, on the top of your closed left fist (**12**).

"It is easier to manipulate the silver balls if I moisten them a little."

Reach across and apparently remove the ball from the top of your left fist (**13**) but, as soon as your fingers shield the ball from view, let it drop back inside your left fist by relaxing the fingers slightly. Immediately remove your right hand as if grasping the ball. Hold the hand in the display position for a second, then "push" your fingers into the corner of your right *eye* as if you were actually pushing the ball into it (**14**). Lower your right hand and show it to be empty (**15**). Blink a few times!

"It hurts at first – but you get used to it!"

Open your left hand and show that it only contains *two* balls (**16**)! One really has gone! Now watch *them* blink! Two balls are now displayed on your left palm.

13

14

15

16

Reach over, as before, apparently removing one but actually removing *two* balls, closing the left fingers as before (**17**). Display your right hand, and once more secretly load a ball into your mouth while apparently only placing a ball between your lips for moistening (**18**). Remove the visible ball and place it on your left fist as before (**19**). Drop it secretly back into your closed left fist in the action of picking it up (**20**). Display your right hand again for a moment and then "push" it into your right ear (**21**)!

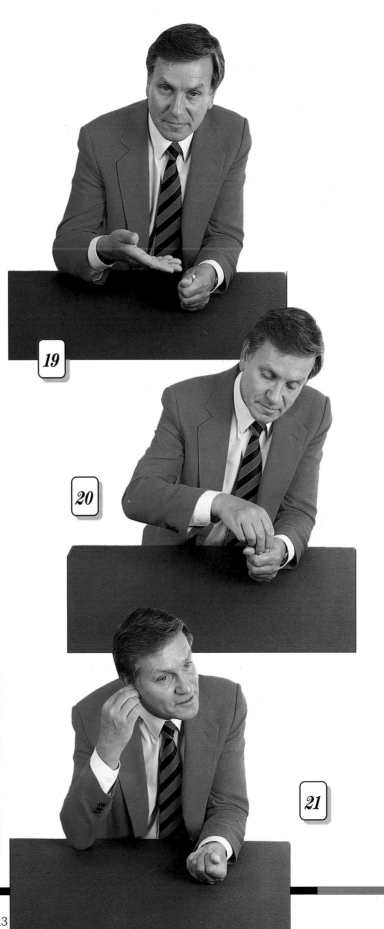

The routine now varies a little. Remove the remaining silver ball with your right hand, duplicating your previous actions when you were secretly removing two balls (**23**). Hold it in the display position. Place it between your lips, moisten it (**24**), then remove it and place it on the top of your left fist exactly as before (**25**). When you reach across for the ball, this time you actually do pick it up! Hold it in the display position for a moment, making sure that the ball is clearly seen (**26**). Now "massage" this ball into the back of your neck (**27**). Actually you quickly push the ball down the back of your shirt collar (**28**) and then continue rhythmically rubbing the back of your neck. After three or four rubs, remove your hand and then show both hands completely empty back and front (**29**).

Pause and smile. Apparently the trick is over. This is the impression that you must give. The position at this stage is that you have two balls concealed in your mouth and one down the back of your collar. You can forget about this last one – you will not be needing it again. Your "pause" should last about six seconds.

"Of course if you want the balls to return, you just rub a little under your chin."

As you do this you push one of the balls forward with your tongue so that it appears between your lips. Your right thumb and index finger rise to remove it (**30**) but, as soon as the ball is masked by your fingers, let it secretly drop back into your mouth again. Remove your right hand as if actually holding the ball and push the ball into your closed left fist (**31**). Rub under your chin again and "regurgitate" another ball so that it is displayed between your lips. Follow the actions exactly as before, apparently removing the ball and pushing it into your fist, when in actual fact you let it drop back into your mouth again. Repeat all these actions for a third time.

Now pause again for a few seconds. Again your audience will think that the trick is over. Take advantage of this. Be "off beat". Apparently you are now holding three balls in your closed left fist. Speak to the nearest spectator:

"Look after the balls for me, please."

As he extends his hand, slowly open your left hand as if to dump the balls on to his palm. Too late! The balls have flown (**32**)!

26

27

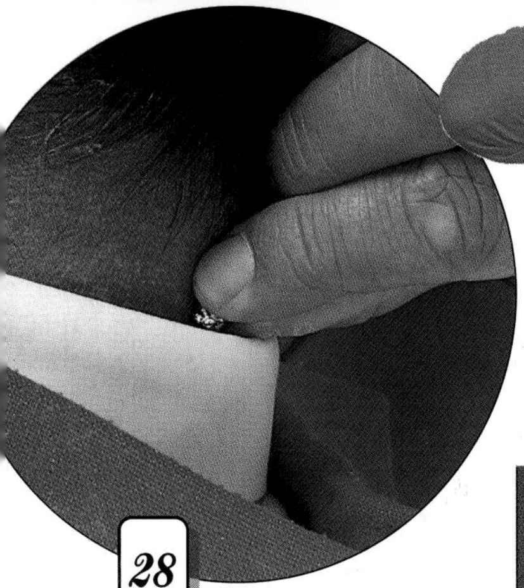

28

29

30

31

32

◆ AFTERTHOUGHTS ◆

Well – that's it. Three great ''climaxes'' plus an absorbing and *extremely* mystifying, close-up, *impromptu* trick. I consider it to be one of the best in my repertoire. What about the two balls still in your mouth? Relax! Nobody knows they are there. Keep them under your tongue until you can dispose of them without being seen.

THE FADE-AWAY PEN

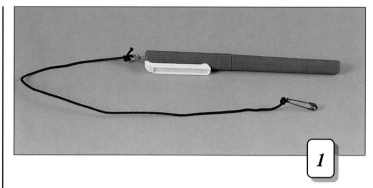

1

In this trick we use a very old principle to create a very modern mystery. Tricks that use "ordinary" everyday objects are always effective because the spectator is familiar with the object and will not expect it suddenly to develop magical properties.

♣ EFFECT ♣

A pen is removed from your inside jacket pocket and shown quite openly. You cover it for a split second with a linen handkerchief and in the space of this split second, it *completely vanishes*! The pen is then reproduced from the jacket pocket from which you originally took it!

REQUIREMENTS
Two identical pens with tops that
screw or clip on firmly
One small screw-eye
30cm of elastic cord
A small safety pin
A linen handkerchief

◆ PREPARATION ◆

One of the pens must be gimmicked beforehand by inserting the small screw-eye in the top of the cap. Onto this you tie 30cm of good quality elastic cord at the end of which you attach the small safety pin (**1**). Place the ungimmicked duplicate pen in your inside left jacket pocket. The gimmicked pen is hung inside your right sleeve. The safety pin fixes inside the jacket near the arm pit. The elastic runs along the inside of the sleeve. The end of the pen should come to rest midway between your elbow and your wrist. If you have allowed too much elastic, adjust it until it hangs correctly. The handkerchief goes over your left arm.

Just before you intend to perform this trick, place your hand casually behind your back. Reach inside your right sleeve with your left fingers. Grasp the end of the pen and pull it down so that you can grip it against your right palm with your right fingers (**2**). You are now ready to perform.

◀ WHAT YOU DO ▶

Reach inside your jacket with your right hand (pen concealed). As soon as your fingers are out of sight gradually work the pen forward until it is held, by the fixed end, between the thumb and fingers. Remove your hand from inside your jacket with the pen openly displayed (**3**). Unscrew the pen with your left fingers and show both parts (backs of hands towards the spectators, (**4**). Screw the pen back into the cap.

Take the handkerchief and hold it, spread out, in your left hand (**5**). Place the end of the pen in about the centre of the handkerchief and then throw the folds over it so that the pen is held by the right hand as in (**6**). With your left hand, grasp the *handkerchief* at the top, *not the pen*, although it should appear that you are holding it too. As soon as your left hand has a grip on the handkerchief, release your hold on the pen and it will fly up (down!) your left sleeve! Now comes a beautiful subtlety! Remove your right hand from beneath the handkerchief and grip it on the outside at about where the bottom of the pen would be if it were still there (**7**). Remove your left hand from the top. Due to the natural stiffness of the handkerchief it looks as if the pen is still there (**8**)! Finally grasp a corner of the handkerchief in each hand, and slowly let the handkerchief open out to show that the pen has completely vanished (**9**)!

This looks very pretty, especially if you hold both hands so that your palms are towards the audience, showing that they are both unmistakably empty. Now, after showing your right hand empty, reach inside your jacket and remove the duplicate pen (**10**). Hold it by the ends exactly as you did the gimmicked one. Unscrew the cap and display the two parts separately. Reassemble the pen (**11**) and hand it and the handkerchief out for examination by the audience.

2

3

8

9

4

5

10

11

6

7

➤ AFTERTHOUGHTS ◄

Please practise this series of moves in front of a mirror until you can perform them smoothly and rhythmically. Let's face it, the trick is a simple one to perform, technically speaking. Therefore the bulk of your efforts should be directed towards a clean and graceful *presentation*. Maybe you will have the opportunity to use the genuine pen earlier. You could lend it to somebody to write something down, mark a coin, etc. He will then remember, when you are performing this trick, that he actually wrote with the pen.

THE CUPS AND BALLS

This is probably the oldest trick in the world. We can trace it back to at least 2,500 years B.C. Most magicians have a version of it in their repertoire, some of them requiring great skill to do. Whenever you see a medieval painting of a fairground or market scene, you will often find a street magician tucked away in a corner performing this trick. Here is a very simplified version which you will enjoy performing.

◀ EFFECT ▶

Paper balls pass through the bottoms of solid cups and appear beneath them – then a ball, placed under a cup, disappears, only to be found beneath another cup some distance away!

REQUIREMENTS
Three paper cups (without handles)
Four paper balls – these can be made from old newspaper, coloured tissue paper etc. All four must look identical
A magic wand

◆ PREPARATION ◆

Nest the three cups together, secretly hiding one of the paper balls in the centre cup. Place the stack on the table and lay the remaining three balls out in a row. The magic wand is on the right (**1**).

♣ WHAT YOU DO ♣

Pick up the three nesting cups from the top in your right hand (**2**). Pull off the bottom cup with your left hand. Turn it *smartly* over and place it mouth downwards on the table to your left (**3**). Keep the mouth of the cup *slightly* turned towards yourself so that the spectator is unable to see into it. Do this naturally and not furtively.

118

Pull off the next cup (**4, 5**) and turn it over smartly, placing it in front of you and to the right of the first cup (**6**). This is an exact duplication of your previous action and, because you turn the cup over smartly, the hidden ball that is in it will not be seen. It now lies on the table hidden under the cup that you have just shown to be empty! Take the last cup in your left hand in exactly the same way and place it, mouth downwards to the right of the other two (**17**). Pick up the first of the visible balls and place it on top of the centre cup (**8**).

"Where is the ball?" "On top of the centre cup." **"No, it's on the bottom! Now watch!"**

Nest the right hand cup on top of the ball and centre cup, and then nest the left hand cup on top of these. Pick up the magic wand and tap the stack once (**9**), then put it down again. Lift up the stack of three cups to show that there is now a ball beneath the bottom one (**10**). Apparently it has penetrated through the cups.

Hold the three cups in your right hand as before. Pull off the bottom cup and place it to the left (**11**). Pull off the next cup and invert it smartly over the ball that has just "appeared" (**12**). Invert the last cup to the right (**13**). Place another ball on the centre cup (**14**) and then restack the cups again. Tap the top one with the magic wand (**15**) and then lift the complete stack to show that there are now two balls beneath it (**16**). Another ball has passed through!

Lay out the cups again. This time you invert the centre cup over both these two balls. Place the remaining ball on top of the centre cup (**17**) and restack. Tap with the wand (**18**) and then lift up the stack to show three balls beneath it! (**19**).

Hold the stack of three cups in your right hand again in the starting position. Pull off the bottom cup and place it to your left. Pull off the next one (**20**) and place it to your far *right*. Place the last cup face downwards in the centre. Lift the two cups nearest to you to show they are empty (**21**), replace them, then place a ball on the *left* cup (**22**) and cover it with the centre one. Tap these two with the wand (**23**) and then lift them up. Act surprised that there is not a ball beneath them (**24**).

"It seems to have disappeared!" Pause and then point to the right hand cup. **"Maybe it is over here! Let's see."**

Lift up the cup and, lo and behold, find the missing ball (**25**)!

11

12

13

14

15

16

17

18

19

20

21

22

23

24

25

❥ AFTERTHOUGHTS ❦

The magic wand is used for the purpose of misdirection. It gives the spectators something else to worry about and helps take their minds off our very simple method. A pencil would do just as well.

This is a very basic Cups and Balls routine. If, as I hope, this book inspires you to take up conjuring as a hobby, you may well learn routines where fruit or money appear beneath the magical cups! The Cups and Balls trick has really stood the test of time!

MIGHTIER THAN THE SWORD

Have you ever wondered what to do with your old newspapers? Here is one answer . . .

✣ EFFECT ✣

A long strip of newspaper is shown on both sides. Boldly and deliberately the strip is cut in half and the two parts displayed separately. They are then placed together, given another snip and then a shake . . . Lo and behold, the two pieces have joined together into one long strip again!

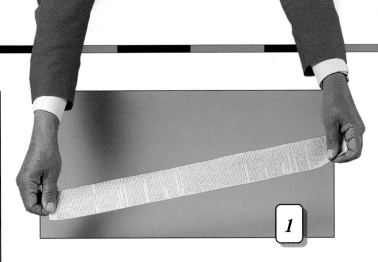

> **REQUIREMENTS**
> A newspaper
> A pair of sharp scissors
> Rubber cement
> Talcum powder

◆ PREPARATION ◆

Cut a long strip of newspaper from the small ads section. Avoid a strip with any distinctive photographs or other bold features. The strip should be at least 50cm long and 5cm wide (**1**). Paint a spread of rubber cement across the centre of the newspaper strip in a band about 5cm wide (**2**). Allow it to dry and then sprinkle talcum powder over the treated area. Blow off any surplus. As I am sure you know, when two surfaces that have been treated with rubber cement come into contact with one another they stick. This is the principle behind self-sealing envelopes. The talcum treatment prevents this from happening prematurely.

➤ WHAT YOU DO ◀

Hold the strip of newspaper up by one end. Fold the strip in half so that the "treated" side goes to the *outside*. Cut the strip in half, through the centre loop (**3**). Display the two halves, one in each hand (**4**). Place both halves together – this time with the treated sections on the *inside* (**5**).

Keeping the two halves aligned, just snip off a couple of millimetres from the ends (**6**). This cutting action has the effect of forcing the rubber cement from each section to weld together along the complete length of the cut edge (**7**). The talcum powder prevents a more widespread adhesion. Let one end of the newspaper drop. The newspaper is restored (**8**)!

4

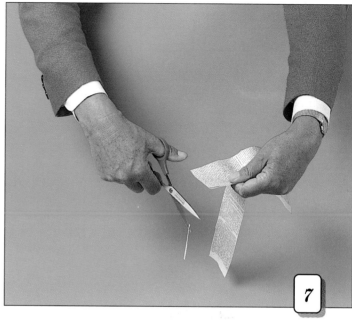

7

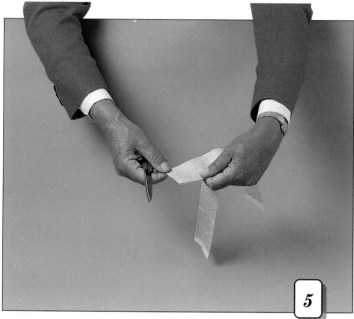

5

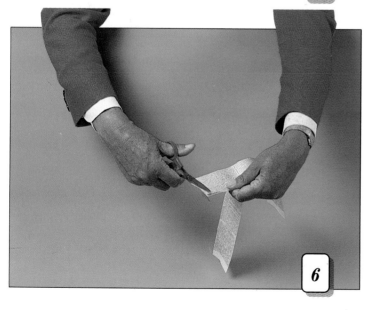

6

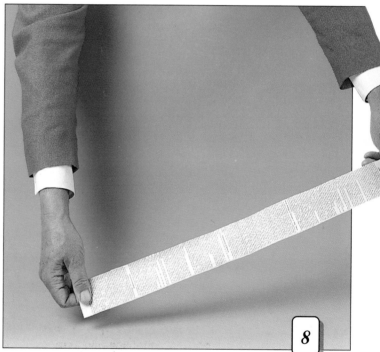

8

← AFTERTHOUGHTS →

I sometimes use this as a "Continuity Gag", picking up the strip between my other tricks and attempting to "do a trick with two pieces of paper". However, the paper keeps joining up again, much to my apparent frustration. After about three attempts at the trick, I finally give up, screw the newspaper into a ball and throw it away in disgust!

FINAL AFTERTHOUGHTS

There are a few general do's and don't's for a magician that I would briefly like to touch upon.

1. Do not overdo it! It is always a mistake to do too many tricks. Four or five knockout tricks should be quite enough for one session. Leave them wanting more.

2. Never divulge your secrets! If someone asks you ". . . how do you do it?" . . . just answer: "Very well!!!" or "It's magic!".

3. Never repeat a trick unless you can create the same effect by using a totally different method. Forewarned is forearmed – if an audience knows *what* is about to happen, there is much more chance that they will discover *how* it happens.

4. People will be watching your hands so make sure that they are clean and well manicured.

5. Practise until you know the trick backwards – until you can perform it in your sleep. The more you practise, the slicker you will become. Practise in front of a mirror so you can see how it looks from the spectator's point of view.

6. Know what you are going to say before you say it. Your patter has to be practised as much as your technique. There is nothing worse than a waffling magician. You could write yourself a script or record it on tape to help you develop a smooth flow.

7. These tricks are described and photographed from a **right-handed** person's point of view. If you are left-handed, just reverse the instructions.

8. Do not try to make your audience look foolish. Some people get annoyed if they cannot work out a trick. Explain beforehand that your object is to *entertain* them. If they knew how you did your tricks, it would not be worth doing them in the first place, would it?!

9. Tricks do sometimes go wrong. It happens to the best of us. Sometimes you will be able to disguise your embarrassment because you very seldom tell an audience what you are going to do until you have done it! If it is not possible, the best policy is to laugh it off and go on to your next trick. Try not to be thrown off your stride by the problem. Find out what went wrong and, at your first opportunity, get in some more practice so that you do not make the same mistake again.

10. Smile! Do not take your newly found skill as a wonderworker too seriously. You will not be entertaining if you do. Nobody likes a smart alec.

My sincere wish in writing these books is to encourage new talent so if, after reading this book, you feel that you would like to progress further, the following notes will be most helpful.

MAGIC CLUBS AND SOCIETIES

Unlike other branches of the entertainment world, magicians seek one another's company and revel in the exchange of ideas. You would do well to join a club (most large towns have one). Space prevents me from mentioning all of them here. These are the main ones:

The Magic Circle
The Players Theatre
Villiers Street
The Strand
London
WC2 6NG

For details write to:
Christopher Pratt, Secretary of The Magic Circle, 13 Calder Avenue, Brookmans Park, Herts, AL9 7AH

International Brotherhood of Magicians
Headquarters
P.O. Box 192090
St. Louis
MO 63119-9998
U.S.A.

The British Ring (No.25) of The International Brotherhood of Magicians can be contacted by writing to: Jeffrey Atkins, The Hon. Secretary, The British Ring I.B.M., Kings Garn, Fritham Court, Fritham, Lyndhurst, Hants, SO43 7HH

British Magical Society
Headquarters
Birmingham and Midland Institute
Margaret Street
Birmingham
B3 3BS

For details write to:
Neil Roberts, Hon. Secretary, British Magical Society,
46 Selby Close, Yardley, Birmingham B26 2AR

The Society of American Magicians
Write to:
John Apperson
S.A.M. Membership Development
2812 Idaho
Granite City
Illinois 62040
U.S.A.

MAGIC MAGAZINES

These keep you up-to-date with the latest news from the world of magic and are essential reading for serious magicians.

Abracadabra (weekly)
Goodliffe Publications Ltd
150 New Road
Bromsgrove
Worcestershire
B60 2LG

Magic (monthly)
Stan Allen & Associates
7380 South Eastern Avenue
Suite 124-179,
Las Vegas
NV 89123
U.S.A.

Genii (monthly)
P.O. Box 36068
Los Angeles
CA 90036
U.S.A.

MAGIC SUPPLIERS

There are many specialist shops around the world which supply the magical fraternity with apparatus and books that are not otherwise available. They all produce catalogues. I list a few below.

L.Davenport & Co
7 Charing Cross Underground Shopping Arcade
The Strand
London
WC2N 4HZ

International Magic Studio
89 Clerkenwell Road
Holborn
London
EC1R 5BX

Magic Books by Post
29 Hill Avenue
Bedminster
Bristol
BS3 4SN

Louis Tannen, Inc.
6 West 32nd Street
4th Floor
New York
N.Y. 10001
U.S.A.

Jeff Busby Magic, Inc.
The Barnard Building
612 Cedar Street
Wallace
Idaho 83873-2233
U.S.A.

If you have enjoyed reading and performing the tricks in this book, you will like its companion volume – *The Amazing Book of Card Tricks* too. It starts by teaching you some simple principles using just an ordinary pack of cards. Then *The Amazing Book of Card Tricks* presents you with two dozen superb tricks that will astound your friends. Each trick has been chosen to enable you, with a little practice, to build up a reputation as somebody not to play cards with!

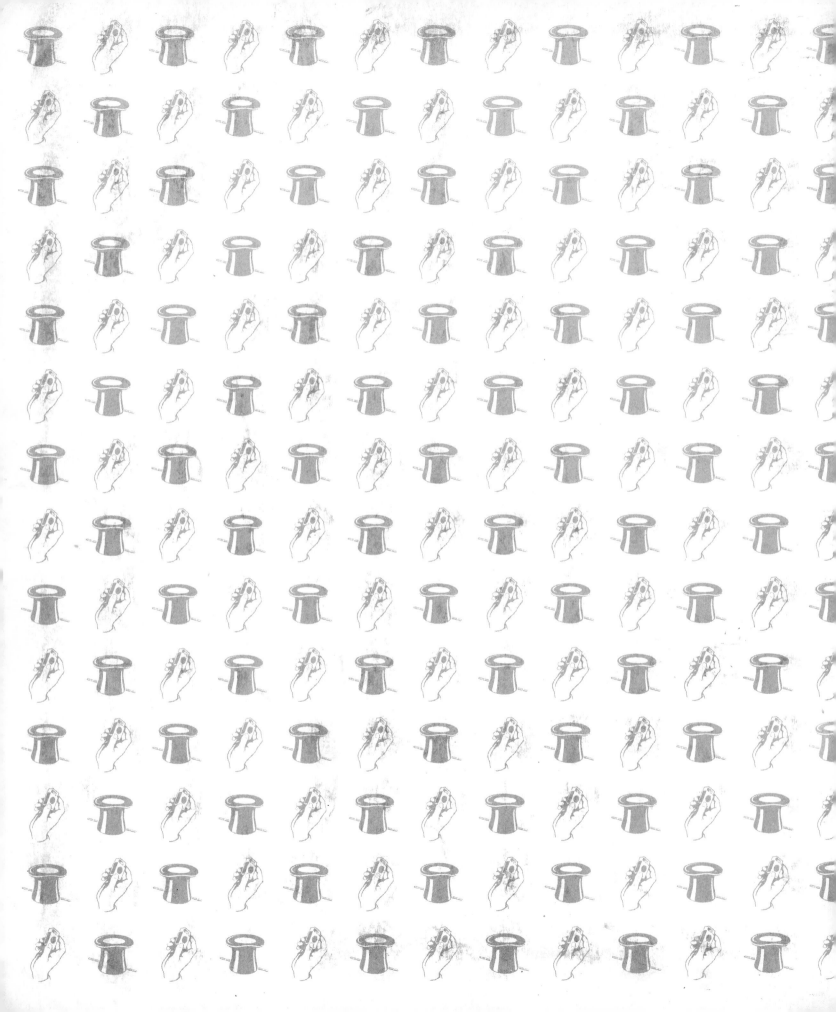